1989

With Love, Lillian

ELVIS
A TRIBUTE
TO
HIS LIFE

CONTRIBUTING WRITER:

SUSAN DOLL

PUBLICATIONS
INTERNATIONAL,
LTD.

Copyright © 1989 Publications International, Ltd.

All rights reserved.

This publication may not be reproduced or quoted
in whole or in part by mimeograph
or any other printed or electronic means, or for
presentation on radio, television,
videotape, or film without
written permission from:

Louis Weber, C.E.O.
Publications International, Ltd.
7373 North Cicero Avenue
Lincolnwood, Illinois 60646
U.S.A.

Permission is never granted for
commercial purposes.

Manufactured in Yugoslavia.

h g f e d c b a

ISBN 0-88176-665-8

Library of Congress Catalog Card
Number: 89-60931

TABLE OF CONTENTS

·

TABLE OF CONTENTS

An image is one thing,

a human being is another.

It's very hard to

live up to an image.

ELVIS PRESLEY

1972

INTRODUCTION

Tupelo is a sleepy southern town in the northeast corner of Mississippi. Locals call the area the Tennessee Hills, but on maps it's clearly the southwestern margin of the Appalachian Mountains. Few people who live outside of these hills would ever have heard of Tupelo if it weren't for the whirlwind born there in 1935. That whirlwind was named Elvis Presley, and he blew out of Tupelo into Memphis and then sped across the country and around the world with a force that's never been equaled. Elvis changed the course of popular music forever, and he also changed the course of our lives. He literally "rocked" the nation.

Elvis was a phenomenally successful performer. He made it big in the recording industry, the movies, television, and live concerts. His fans remember Elvis in many different ways, and *Elvis: A Tribute to His Life* is full of cherished images of Elvis. Like an album filled with much-loved family photos, this book remembers his extraordinary life and career. It is a tribute to the young Elvis, who held the nation captive with his electrifying performing style; to Elvis the movie star, who entertained the whole family with his charming portrayals of romantic leading men; and to Elvis in concert, who ripped Las Vegas wide open with his explosive live performances.

Elvis is one of the United States' most celebrated entertainers, but he is more than a star. In Elvis's story we see something original and exciting, something wild and excessive. Maybe we even see ourselves. Fans are fascinated by the most minute details of Elvis's life, and this obsession goes far beyond our usual interest in popular entertainers. The actual events of Elvis's life formed the plots of many of his movies and the lyrics of some of his songs. The strength and power of his image are inseparable from his personal life. Much that has been written about Elvis distorts the facts to enhance their publicity value. Other mistakes have been caused by over-eager writers accepting hearsay as fact. Details often vary and versions of a single event are endlessly reinterpreted. Elvis has become a legendary figure, and while we honor him in every way, our tribute to Elvis is as straightforward as it can possibly be. This book retells the familiar stories, but it also explains contradictions and gets to the plain truth behind the legend.

CHAPTER ONE

HUMBLE BEGINNINGS

Elvis and his mother came in one morning.

He was anxious to buy a rifle; his mother was trying to persuade him

to buy a guitar.

I showed him the rifle first and then I took him and

showed him his guitar. . . .

He told his mother he didn't have enough money to buy the guitar

and so she said,

"I'll pay up for you, but I can't pay up if it's

to buy a rifle."

F. L. BOBO

On January 8, 1935, Gladys Presley gave birth to twin sons. Her first baby, Jessie Garon, was stillborn. A half hour later his twin, Elvis Aron, was born. There's no medical evidence that the twins were identical, but both Elvis and his mother believed that they were. The death of his twin had a profound effect on Elvis for his entire life. He was fascinated by his unknown brother and saddened by the loss of the twin he always believed was his exact double.

Elvis's twin brother, Jessie Garon, is buried in an unmarked grave in Priceville Cemetery, located just north of Tupelo. The actual gravesite is known to only a handful of people.

Confusion over the correct spelling of Elvis's middle name has existed since his birth, when the physician attending Gladys scribbled "Aaron" on Elvis's birth certificate. Photographs of his official birth certificate issued by the state of Mississippi show the spelling "Aron," which is also found on his draft notice. But his gravestone in Meditation Gardens at Graceland is engraved with the more common spelling "Aaron." Biographers of Elvis Presley disagree about the correct spelling of his middle name, but his ex-wife, Priscilla Presley, who is the biographer closest to Elvis, used "Aaron" in her bittersweet chronicle of their life together.

While the truth may never be known, it's likely that Gladys intended the spelling "Elvis Aron" to match "Jessie Garon." Relatives and neighbors have said that Gladys knew throughout her pregnancy that she was going to have twins. She undoubtedly selected their names to honor family members. Elvis was named after his father, Vernon Presley, whose middle name was Elvis, and Jessie was the name of Vernon's father. But there's little doubt that Gladys also chose the names because they sounded alike. She wanted her perfectly matched boys to have perfectly matched names.

Vernon and Gladys Presley had been married for about a year and a half when Elvis was born. The couple met in the spring of 1933, and after a two-month courtship they were married. They may have rushed into marriage because they hoped to escape the miserable situations in which they had been living and build a better life together. At the time of their marriage, Vernon was 17 and Gladys was 21, but they both lied about their ages on the marriage license. She said she was 19, and he claimed to be 22.

After a whirlwind courtship, Vernon Elvis Presley and Gladys Love Smith were married in 1933. A year and a half later, Elvis was born.

In his short life Vernon had already experienced many ups and downs. He must not have had a close relationship with his father, Jessie, because his dad kicked Vernon out of the house when he was only 15. Despite the friction between father and son, Vernon was his mother's favorite child. Minnie Mae Presley had four other children, but she always depended on Vernon. When he took his wife and son to live in Memphis, Minnie Mae moved in with them, leaving the mean-tempered Jessie behind in Tupelo. Ironically, Minnie outlived both her favorite son and her famous grandson.

Vernon's life was filled with hardship and poverty, but Gladys's life was even worse. Gladys Love Smith was born in Pontotoc County, Mississippi, which was deep in the backwoods compared to Tupelo, where Vernon grew up. Gladys had seven brothers and sisters. Her father, who was a sharecropper and possibly a moonshiner, died when Gladys was a teenager. She had to go to work to help support her family because her mother was frail and sick. Gladys was an attractive girl; she was tall and thin, and had dark hair and eyes. But throughout her life she was often melancholy. Her unhappiness may have been caused by all the misfortune she had to cope with at such an early age.

When the Smith family moved to Tupelo, Gladys met Vernon Presley. After they were married, Vernon built a house for his bride on land belonging to a farmer named Orville S. Bean. The two-room house is only 15 feet wide and 30 feet long. This kind of sharecropper's house is known as a "shotgun shack," because if you shot a bullet through the front door, it would go straight through the house and out the back door without hitting anything. Elvis was born in this primitive house in a community where it wasn't unusual for bullets to fly through the front door.

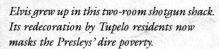

Elvis grew up in this two-room shotgun shack. Its redecoration by Tupelo residents now masks the Presleys' dire poverty.

After Elvis became a star and the house became a tourist attraction, some local residents took great care to turn the shack into what you might call a quaint bungalow. They painted the outside, wallpapered the walls, and hung curtains at the windows. The struggling young Presley family could never have afforded any of this. The house has also been furnished with a high chair, a sewing machine, and some electric appliances, although when the Presleys lived there, the electricity was not even hooked up. A swing was added to the porch, and the front yard was landscaped. The fresh paint and bright furnishings conceal the true poverty in which Elvis grew up, as well as his family's lack of social status. Their abject poverty has been upgraded to seem like "humble beginnings" for the sake of the tourists and the "official" Elvis Presley life story as it appeared in newspapers and fan magazines.

Wallpaper, curtains, and an old-fashioned high chair—simple comforts the Presleys could never have afforded—were added to the interior of the shack after it was designated a state historical site.

Vernon Presley held odd jobs before and after Elvis was born. He worked as a sharecropper for Orville S. Bean (on whose land his home was built), drove a milk truck, and made deliveries for several grocery stores. In 1937 Vernon was convicted of forgery along with Travis Smith and Luther Gable, and sentenced to three years in prison. In 1938 he was sent to Parchman Penitentiary, which was a cotton plantation that had been turned into a prison farm, where the inmates worked the land in chain gangs. The sentence seems harsh considering the crime: Vernon, Smith, and Gable had altered the figures on a check to Vernon from Orville Bean. No one knows the exact amount of money involved, but most people believe it was quite small.

Although an electric light now burns brightly in the bedroom of Elvis's humble birthplace, the Presleys did not have the luxury of electricity while they were living there.

Gladys began working at the Tupelo Garment Factory before her marriage, and she continued to work there until her pregnancy became troublesome. When Elvis was a few months old, she went out to pick cotton, hauling her baby on a cotton sack as she moved up and down the rows. After Vernon was sent to prison, Bean turned Gladys and Elvis out of their house. They moved in with Vernon's parents, and Gladys took in laundry and worked as a seamstress to support herself and Elvis.

There are many versions of the story of Elvis's childhood, but they all agree that Gladys and Elvis were unusually close. Biographers have been told by many people that Gladys did not want to leave her son in the care of anyone else for any length of time. She seems to have been overprotective and would even defend Elvis with a broom if an older boy tried to pick on him. Gladys also insisted on walking Elvis to and from school until he was a teenager. Gladys set goals for her son. She was determined that he would get the education that she and Vernon never had. Walking Elvis to school every day assured her that at least her son attended school regularly. Gladys's protective nature and close bond with her son seem easy to understand, since he was her only child. Jessie Garon had died at birth, and later Gladys suffered at least one miscarriage. Finally, her doctor told her that she would never be able to have any more children. During the difficult time when Vernon was in prison, Gladys must have turned to Elvis for support, and their relationship naturally became much closer than it might have in other circumstances.

A devastating tornado on April 6, 1936, may also have contributed to Gladys's special feeling about the preciousness of her son. Elvis was just 15 months old when a tornado hit Tupelo, killing more than 200 people and injuring 500. The twister totally destroyed the black neighborhood Tank Hill. The courthouse, many churches, and even movie theaters were converted into temporary hospitals. President Franklin D. Roosevelt sent federal aid, and the Red Cross was called in to assist people whose homes had been demolished. That fateful night, the Presleys had gone home from church with Elvis's Great-Uncle Noah, so they were at his house when the storm hit. When Vernon and Gladys ventured out and returned to their home, they discovered that the tornado had flattened St. Mark's Methodist Church across the road from their house, but had left their tiny home untouched. They must have been genuinely thankful for what little they had.

This grade-school photo captures Elvis (far right in the second row from the top) dressed in the denim overalls he would later despise.

During the Depression the people in Tupelo, like people everywhere, relied on family and neighbors for help during times of extreme economic hardship. Elvis not only felt a deep bond for his mother, but he was also close to his aunts, uncles, and cousins. After he became successful, he took care of many of them financially, just as some of them had taken care of Gladys and him.

The Presleys belonged to the First Assembly of God, a Pentecostal church that believes in faith healing and baptism conferring the gift of speaking in tongues. Many biographers attribute Elvis's flamboyant performing style to the influence of this emotionally expressive church, although the connection may be somewhat exaggerated. Elvis referred often to singing in this little church for a congregation of about 25 people. He also remembered watching impassioned preachers lead services. But the exact nature of the church's influence on him is unknown. No one has said that any of the Presleys experienced a dramatic religious conversion, although later in his life Vernon became a deacon in the church.

As a child, Elvis closely resembled his mother, Gladys.

Many of Elvis's biographers don't have much to say about his amateur musical experiences outside of the church. Perhaps no one wants to shatter the "official" version of Elvis's discovery, which maintains it was only by chance that the young man walked into Sam Phillips's recording studio in 1953 to become a star. But even before he moved to Memphis, Elvis was interested in country music and had begun performing.

In 1945, at the age of ten, Elvis sang on the radio for the first time. He won second prize at the annual Mississippi-Alabama Fair and Dairy Show for singing "Old Shep," a ballad about a boy and his dog that was made popular by country singer Red Foley. The show was broadcast live over Tupelo radio station WELO. Elvis's prize was free admission to all the rides at the fair and five dollars.

That same year, Elvis had gotten his first guitar. It was his tenth-birthday present from his parents. Some people say that he actually wanted a bicycle, but his family couldn't afford one, so his mother bought him a guitar instead. But F.L. Bobo, who operated the Tupelo Hardware Company, where Gladys bought the guitar, insisted that Elvis really wanted a rifle. Not surprisingly, Gladys felt that a gun was too dangerous and insisted on getting him a guitar. Before Bobo died, he signed an affidavit stating his version of the story. The document now hangs on the second floor of the hardware store.

Elvis learned to play the guitar from his father's brother, Vester Presley, who joined Elvis's parents in encouraging the boy's musical talent. Even before Elvis appeared at the Mississippi-Alabama Fair, he had been singing with his mom and dad at churches, camp meetings, and revivals. Elvis's first biographies and album-cover notes confirm that he was singing in public when he was only nine years old.

It's possible that Elvis also sang on the amateur radio program *Black and White Jamboree* (also called *Saturday Jamboree*) on Tupelo station WELO. The program had a live studio audience, and anyone could sing in front of the mike; you just had to wait in line. Elvis attended the show regularly, and he may have sung "Old Shep" on the air when he was as young as eight or nine before he made his well-documented radio debut at the fair.

The interior of the Tupelo Hardware Company, where Gladys bought Elvis his first guitar, reflects the atmosphere of an old country store.

Elvis learned about traditional country music from Mississippi Slim, whose real name was Carvel Lee Ausborn. Slim was a native of Tupelo, and he sang on WELO for more than 20 years. He made only a few recordings, including "Honky Tonk Woman," "Tired of Your Eyes," and "I'm Through Crying Over You," but Slim is remembered as the epitome of the "hillbilly" singer. Elvis heard Slim perform many times on *Jamboree*, and Slim may have taught the boy several new chords on the guitar. Elvis's interest in Mississippi Slim indicates that he was an aspiring performer before he moved to Memphis. If you look beyond the limited view of many of Elvis's biographers, you'll find that his music was influenced by gospel and traditional country singers as well as the blues and rhythm-and-blues performers he encountered after he left Tupelo.

A sworn affidavit by F.L. Bobo, who sold Elvis that first guitar, now hangs on the second floor of the Tupelo Hardware Company. The document relates Bobo's version of this legendary Elvis tale.

CHAPTER TWO

THE MEMPHIS SOUND

He used to come around and be around us a lot.

There was a place we used to go and hang out at on Beale Street.

People had little pawn shops there and a lot of us used to

hang around in certain of these places,

and this was where I met him.

B. B. KING

The Presley family moved from Tupelo to Memphis in September 1948, just after Elvis started high school. Vernon had gotten a factory job in Memphis during World War II, but returned to Tupelo in 1947 and went to work again as a delivery man. Most people believe that the Presleys decided to move to Memphis because Vernon couldn't find a good job in Tupelo. For whatever reason, the family, along with Vernon's mother, Minnie Mae, left town quickly and quietly.

For the next four years the Presleys lived in the slums of Memphis. After a brief stay in a one-room apartment in a boarding house, they moved into the federal housing project at Lauderdale Courts. By the end of 1952 both Gladys and Vernon were working, and the family's income exceeded the maximum allowed by the Memphis Housing Authority. The Presleys were forced to leave the housing project, but they chose to remain in the Lauderdale Courts neighborhood, where they lived until Elvis became successful and bought them a house in a better part of town.

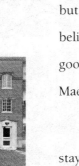

The Lauderdale Courts housing project was home to the Presleys for more than three years.

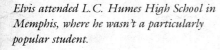

Elvis attended L.C. Humes High School in Memphis, where he wasn't a particularly popular student.

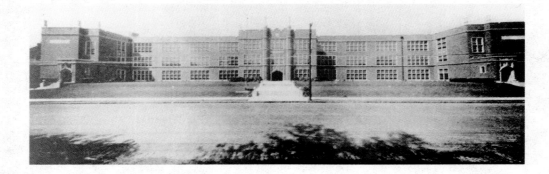

Elvis attended L.C. Humes High School, where he majored in industrial arts/woodshop. While he was in school, Elvis had many part-time jobs, including ushering at Loew's State Theater. He became a target of ridicule from some of his fellow students because of his unusual appearance. When he was 16, Elvis grew his hair longer than the other boys and greased it down with pomade. He started dressing in flashy clothes: brightly colored shirts turned up at the collar and baggy gabardine slacks pegged at the bottom. This style, which had started in the big cities in the North, was popular with Memphis's black rhythm-and-blues musicians. Elvis graduated from Humes in 1953 and went to work at Crown Electric as a truck driver. It's been said that he brought home about $41 per week.

This ad was used by Crown Electric in the Yellow Pages of the Memphis telephone book.

PHILLIPS, JAMES ARNETT
Major: Science, Special Studies, Drafting, English.
Activities: Thespian, National Forensic, Debate Team, Spanish Club, Hi-Y Biology Club, History Club, Speech Club, Student Council Representative, Non-Com Officer in R. O. T. C., Vice-President Speech Club, Vice-President History Club.
Awards: Winner District Debate Tournament, Winner "I Speak For Democracy" Contest.

ROBINSON, KATIE MAE
Major: Commercial, Home Ec., English.
Activities: F. H. A., History Club, English Club, Vice-President History Club.

RULEMAN, SHIRLEY
Major: Home Ec., Commercial, English.
Activities: National Honor Society, F. H. A., Y-Teens, Latin Club, Jr. Cheerleader, Sabre Club, History Club, English Club, Honorary Captain in R. O. T. C., President Home Ec. Class.

PRESLEY, ELVIS ARON
Major: Shop, History, English.
Activities: R. O. T. C., Biology Club, English Club, History Club, Speech Club.

PERRY, ROBERT EARL
Major: History, Science, English.
Activities: Biology Club, T&I Club, Key Club, Baseball 4 years, Vice-President Key Club, Boys' Vice-President Senior Class, President T&I Club.
Awards: All-Star American Legion Baseball Team 1952, National Honor Society.

SANDERS, MARY LOUISE
Major: Commercial, Band, English.
Activities: Senior Band, Y-Teens, English Club, History Club, Historian of Band.

SEALY, CAROLYN NAOMI
Major: Commercial, Art, English.
Activities: Fifty Club, Y-Teens, Red Cross, Monitor, Sight-Saving Room.
Award: Merit Award in Lion Oil Essay Contest, Scholastic Golden Key Award in Art.

ROTENBERRY, JAMES RUSSELL
Major: Drafting, Shop, English.
Activities: History Club, English Club, Biology Club, Hi-Y Science Club, President Science Club, Vice-President Biology Club.

ROBINSON, EDWARD McMILLAN
Major: Math, Drafting, English.
Activities: Biology Club, History Club, Rifle Team, English Club, Student Council Representative.

SEXTON, BONNIE
Major: Commercial, Home Ec., English.
Activities: F. H. A., Y-Teens, Red Cross, Student Council, Honor Society, Herald Staff, Secretary F. H. A., Vice-President Red Cross, Secretary Senior Class.
Awards: Attended F. H. A. Convention in Nashville.

SLATE, SHIRLEY
Major: Commercial, English.

Although often mistakenly identified as Elvis's prom night, this photo actually shows Elvis and girlfriend Dixie Locke at Locke's prom in the spring of 1954.

His senior picture from the 1953 Herald, the Humes High School yearbook, shows that Elvis preferred to slick back his hair with pomade long before he became a professional rocker.

Elvis poses with his beloved parents.

Although the influences on Elvis's music during this period of his life are not fully documented, he is known to have listened to all-night gospel sings and to the wide variety of music available on Memphis radio stations, especially WDIA and WHBQ. Station WDIA broadcast black music. It was owned by two white men, Bert Ferguson and John R. Pepper, but staffed with black disc jockeys who played the blues, with a special emphasis on Memphis's own blues artists. WHBQ was a white station that played a variety of music, but it's best remembered for disc jockey Dewey Phillips's *Red Hot and Blue* program, which featured the rhythm-and-blues recordings of black artists.

Memphis was the headquarters for white gospel music in the 1950s. During 1951 and 1952 Elvis frequently attended all-night gospel sings at Ellis Auditorium. Male quartets often headlined at these sings, and Elvis's favorite groups included the Blackwood Brothers and the Statesmen. The lead singer of this quartet was the colorful Jake Hess. Many people remember the Statesmen for their emotional, highly stylized singing and flamboyant wardrobes, and undoubtedly they made an impression on young Elvis.

The Blackwood Brothers attended the same Assembly of God church as the Presleys, and along with their junior quartet called the Songbirds, they were probably a major influence on Elvis. Cecil Blackwood, the youngest Blackwood brother and a member of the Songbirds, was in Elvis's Sunday school class. After he left the junior quartet to join his brothers as part of the Blackwoods, Cecil suggested that Elvis join the Songbirds. For some reason, nothing ever came of this opportunity.

The Blackwood Brothers, a gospel quartet that was a major musical influence on Elvis, performed regularly at all-night sings and church get-togethers in the Memphis area.

Accounts of Elvis's life from family members and close friends, including Priscilla Presley and Red and Sonny West, confirm that his love of gospel music was a major influence on his singing and performance style. But other accounts of Elvis's career emphasize his connection with Memphis's famed Beale Street. The clubs in this seedy area were home to many well-known rhythm-and-blues musicians. According to some accounts of Elvis's life, he frequented Beale Street, eventually taking up the sound he heard there as his own. But even though Elvis was known to visit the clubs on Beale Street, he may have learned just as much about the blues and rhythm and blues from listening to the radio.

Elvis was acquainted with many rhythm-and-blues artists in Memphis, including B.B. King, Rufus Thomas, and Big Memphis Ma Rainey. King was a disc jockey at that time, and he recalls running into Elvis on Beale Street and seeing him hanging around the clubs and pawn shops. Elvis bought most of his flamboyant wardrobe at the Lansky brothers' clothing store, located at the end of Beale Street.

The great bluesman B.B. King was a disc jockey in Memphis during the early 1950s. He recalls seeing Elvis on Beale Street at that time.

The country influence on Elvis's music often takes a back seat to the more colorful Beale Street stories. Elvis's friend, country singer Mississippi Slim, taught him a lot about country music back in Tupelo, and Elvis often listened to one of Memphis's country radio stations. Gladys Presley loved to listen to the radio and was a big fan of country artist Hank Snow. Elvis grew up with country music, listening to the radio with his mother.

The style and sound of country music changed during the 1940s. Ernest Tubb brought electric guitars to the *Grand Ole Opry*, and boogie-woogie was fused with country into a new sound called "western swing." The enormous popularity of Hank Williams, whose sound had been influenced by the blues, also began to affect the sound of country music. By the early 1950s, some of the fans and many members of the country music establishment had not yet embraced these innovations, but Elvis must have enjoyed the new sound because he incorporated and expanded it in his music.

Elvis picked up his hip attire at the Lansky brothers' clothing store on Beale Street.

Elvis's unique singing and performing style is a fusion of gospel, country, and rhythm and blues, with a little pop thrown in here and there. No single musical influence is more important than another. His music is a true integration of contemporary music styles into a totally new sound.

CHAPTER THREE

HILLBILLY CAT

If I could find a white man

who had the Negro sound and the Negro feel,

I could make a billion dollars.

SAM PHILLIPS

AROUND 1953

What really happened on the summer day in 1953 when Elvis Presley entered Sam Phillips's Memphis Recording Service has been lost to history, but there's plenty of speculation and lots of tall tales have been told about Elvis's discovery. The most-often-told tale begins with a shy, 18-year-old Elvis entering a recording studio to cut two songs on an acetate disk for his mother's birthday at a cost of four dollars. Since Gladys's birthday is in April, the timing in this story is way off because everyone agrees that Elvis made his first acetate disk in the late summer of 1953. It's more likely that Elvis knew of Philips's reputation as an independent producer and was trying to catch his attention.

No one has to wonder if Sun Studio is legendary in the history of rock 'n' roll. It says so right on the sign!

Sam Phillips not only owned and operated the Memphis Recording Service, he also owned Sun Records, an independent record label that had been recording rhythm-and-blues artists since 1950. By the time Elvis came to the recording studio, Phillips was known as Memphis's most important independent record producer. He also enjoyed a national reputation for discovering talented R&B artists. Phillips recorded these performers for independent record companies in other parts of the United States, including Chess Records in Chicago and the Modern label in Los Angeles. Phillips financed the recording sessions, paid the musicians, recorded the artists himself (often serving as the studio engineer), and then leased the master recordings to other record companies. Phillips's reputation was built on his recordings of R&B performers, but he had just begun to work with country singers when Elvis walked into his recording studio for the first time.

Unfortunately, on the day Elvis decided to step into the Memphis Recording Service, Phillips was not there. His tireless secretary and assistant, Marion Keisker, was running the recording studio alone. She noticed Elvis's flamboyant clothes and his long, slicked-back hair, and decided to find out who this cool guy was. Keisker asked Elvis what kind of music he sang and who he sounded like. His prophetic answer, "I don't sound like nobody," piqued her curiosity, so while Elvis was singing "My Happiness" by the Ink Spots for his record, Keisker also taped him on newly invented magnetic tape so that Phillips could hear him later.

Sam Phillips, the man who discovered and helped develop Elvis's unique singing style, was already a well-established record producer when Elvis walked through the door of his studio.

(From left to right) Jerry Lee Lewis, Carl Perkins, Elvis, and Johnny Cash all recorded on the Sun label. On December 4, 1956, these four legends of rockabilly recorded together. The songs were not released until much later in their careers, at which time the four were dubbed the Million Dollar Quartet.

The Hillbilly Cat and the Blue Moon Boys: Bill Black, Elvis, and Scotty Moore.

In the early 1950s, rhythm and blues, or R&B, was a new sound that combined urban blues with swing. It was called "race music" because almost all R&B musicians were black. Phillips felt that rhythm and blues could win a mass audience if he could find a white man who could sing with the sound and feel of a black man. According to Marion Keisker, everyone in Memphis knew what Phillips was looking for. So Elvis's choice of another Ink Spots number, "That's When Your Heartaches Begin," for the flip side of his first acetate was probably intended to show Phillips that he had a black sound. The experienced producer listened to the two songs by the unknown singer, but he didn't do anything about them, even though legend would have it that Elvis's natural talent immediately blew Sam Phillips away.

Years later, after Elvis had become a major star, Phillips changed the story a little. He claimed that he was the person behind the desk at the Memphis Recording Service on that landmark day. To support his claim, Phillips points out that Marion Keisker didn't know how to operate the recording equipment, so he was the only person who could have recorded Elvis. But Marion Keisker told her version of the story many times in print and during television interviews, and as far as anyone knows, Elvis never disputed her facts.

Even though nothing came of his first session at the Memphis Recording Service, Elvis was determined to give it another shot. He returned to the studio in January 1954 to record two more songs on acetate. He sang "Casual Love Affair" and a country tune, "I'll Never Stand in Your Way." This time Phillips worked the controls. He offered the young singer little encouragement, but he took Elvis's phone number and address.

Phillips didn't call Elvis until Peer Music sent him a demo record of the ballad "Without You." Phillips decided to allow Elvis to record the new ballad, but Elvis could not seem to master the song, so Phillips asked him to sing anything else he knew. Delighted with the opportunity, Elvis eagerly ran through his extensive repertoire of country songs and R&B tunes. Phillips was impressed and suggested that he get together with Scotty Moore, a young guitarist who played with a local country combo called the Starlight Wranglers. Moore introduced Elvis to bass player Bill Black, and the three musicians spent the long, hot Memphis summer trying to find a sound that clicked.

This early publicity shot from 1954 shows little of the confidence and charisma Elvis would develop after just a few months on the road.

The trio worked together in the recording studio at Sun Records instead of performing in front of a live audience. Recently developed magnetic recording tape made it possible for them to do one take of a song, listen to it, and then make adjustments for the next take. Presley, Moore, and Black finally hit upon their sound while they were fooling around during a break one night. Elvis started singing Arthur "Big Boy" Crudup's blues song, "That's All Right (Mama)," with a fast rhythm and in a more casual style than most blues songs, and Moore and Black jumped right in. Phillips's voice boomed out from the control booth, "What are you doing?" None of them really knew. How could they? How could they know that they had stumbled onto a new sound for a new generation?

Elvis's first recording was a history-making version of Arthur "Big Boy" Crudup's "That's All Right."

Phillips was excited about the trio's sound and recognized its potential. He asked them to refine their unique interpretation of "That's All Right," and then he recorded it. The flip side for their first record was their version of the bluegrass standard "Blue Moon of Kentucky." Elvis's first record shows clearly where his music was coming from; there's a blues song on one side and a country song on the other. Elvis's treatment of the songs didn't sound much like the recordings of the original artists. His approach was more easygoing and gave his renditions an air of spontaneity. He changed the hard vocal delivery and tense rhythm of Crudup's version of "That's All Right" and instead used a more relaxed vocal style and rhythm. For "Blue Moon of Kentucky" Elvis sped up the tempo and added two elements for which he would become famous: He syncopated certain lyrics, using an almost hiccuping sound; and he added reverberation, resulting in an echo effect. Elvis's new sound eventually became known as "rockabilly," because it was the fusion of country music (commonly called hillbilly music) with a rhythm-and-blues beat that had been relaxed and speeded up, or "rocked." The word "rockabilly" was coined long after Elvis had become a household word, and at the time he began to record, there was no term that could describe his music. When the press attempted to explain his sound, they usually made a mess of it, confusing the issue with inappropriate or comical comparisons with other kinds of music.

Sam Phillips took a copy of "That's All Right" to popular disc jockey Dewey Phillips (no relation). He was initially hesitant about airing the song on his radio program *Red Hot and Blue* because he usually played only black artists on his show.

This photo perfectly captures Elvis's explosive performing style.

But Phillips liked what he heard and eventually aired the record. The station received dozens of requests for both sides of the disk, and Phillips played the two songs over and over. The response was so great that he decided to put the unknown singer on his program that same night. Elvis is said to have been too nervous to stay at home and listen to himself on the radio, so he went to the movies. Vernon and Gladys had to pick him up at the theater and then rush him to station WHBQ. Dewey Phillips asked him lots of questions about his life and his interests. But the most significant piece of information revealed during the live interview was the name of the high school Elvis had attended. When Elvis said "Humes," the audience knew that he was white because at that time Humes was an all-white school; in 1954 Memphis schools were not yet integrated.

"That's All Right" became a fast-selling record in Memphis, and by the end of July 1954 it was shooting up the country charts. On July 30, Elvis Presley made his debut as a professional entertainer at Overton Park in Memphis. Singer-yodeler Slim Whitman was on the same bill. Scotty Moore accompanied Elvis on guitar, and Bill Black was on stand-up, or doghouse, bass. Elvis was so new to the music scene that one newspaper ad billed him as "Ellis Presley."

Elvis was 19 years old and as nervous as a cat for the opening show. His nerves and inexperience may explain why he moved constantly while he was singing. Elvis swung his hips and moved his legs in a way that would later cause a scandal. The audience screamed enthusiastically as he danced, shook, and gyrated across the stage. When he finished, Elvis ran offstage and turned to Moore to ask what in the world the audience had been hollering at. Moore laughed, "It was your leg, man! It was the way you were shakin' your left leg."

Elvis's biographers are always trying to figure out which performer Elvis was copying with his legendary performing style. The truth is that his style, with its sensual hip movements and frenetic leg shaking, integrated all the influences on his music, including rhythm and blues, black and white gospel, and country music. In Elvis's performances you can see a little of the white gospel singer Jake Hess of the Statesmen and also the flamboyant preaching style of Pentecostal ministers. He may have gotten his wiggles from the rhythm-and-blues musicians on Beale Street, especially Ukulele Ike, who played the blues at the Gray Mule. But the sources of his techniques aren't

At the beginning of his career, Elvis often performed on the same bill with mainstream country singers.
In August 1955 he appeared with Bill Strength at Overton Park in Memphis.

really important. Elvis was a masterful performer with a stunning style that was ultimately all his own. Later, when Elvis began performing for mainstream audiences, there was a lot of controversy about his unique performing style. But early in his career, little mention was made of his shakes and shimmies. Elvis's promotional material describes him as a hot young country singer with a crazy new sound.

Elvis's second record was released on September 25, 1954. It included a 1948 R&B hit by Wyonie Harris called "Good Rockin' Tonight" and the country pop song "I Don't Care if the Sun Don't Shine." This record began to move up the charts even more quickly than his first single. It sold 4,000 copies in the Memphis area in two-and-a-half weeks.

In September 1954 Elvis was invited to perform on the oldest and most successful country music radio program in America, the *Grand Ole Opry*. Since the *Opry* had always been reluctant to accept changes in country music, including the use of electric guitars and drums, it's not surprising that Elvis's highly charged performance and blues-inspired music were not well received. At that time there was no place for Elvis's music except the country charts, and both Elvis and Sam Phillips were perplexed and disappointed by the reaction to Elvis's performance. The talent coordinator of the *Opry*, Jim Denny, went so far as to suggest that Elvis go back to driving a truck.

Although Elvis's failure to impress *Opry* officials was a setback to his career, he still had many fans in the country-western audience. In October Elvis performed for the first time on *Louisiana Hayride*, a radio program broadcast from Shreveport, Louisiana. The *Hayride*, unlike the *Opry*, had always encouraged new country talent, including Hank Williams, Slim Whitman, Jim Reeves, and Webb Pierce. The Hillbilly Cat and the Blue Moon Boys (as Elvis, Scotty Moore, and Bill Black had begun calling themselves) were so well received on the *Hayride* that they were offered a one-year contract to perform every weekend. The show paid only scale wages, but it gave the trio valuable exposure to country fans all over the country. Even though they now had a regular gig, Elvis and his combo still spent lots of time on the road, often playing off the back of a pick-up truck, earning a meager living, and trying to find their audience.

Elvis did not feel financially secure enough to quit his job at Crown Electric until November 1954. Vernon had always told his son that he'd never met a guitarist who was

Elvis performed on the Grand Ole Opry *when it was located in the old Ryman Auditorium in Nashville.*

Elvis exploded onto Louisiana Hayride, *a radio program broadcast from Shreveport, Louisiana. There he enjoyed his first major success.*

Country superstar Hank Williams achieved acclaim outside the country-western market, setting a precedent for Elvis's breakthrough in 1956.

Country yodeler Slim Whitman shared the bill when Elvis made his public debut at Overton Park in July 1954.

Country crooner Jim Reeves appeared with Elvis several times on Louisiana Hayride.

Back in 1955, the Hillbilly Cat and the Blue Moon Boys had no idea of the significance of their unique sound. It was the perfect blend of black rhythm and blues and country; it was a musical milestone; it was rock 'n' roll.

worth a damn, so Elvis wanted to achieve some success with his music before giving up his steady job. So they'd be sure to have enough work to keep them going, Elvis, Scotty, and Bill decided to hire a manager. Bob Neal, a disc jockey at country station WMPS in Memphis, took the job and began pushing their Sun recordings, booking tours in country-western clubs across the South and Southwest, and handling all their business arrangements.

Elvis warms up on the piano before a live appearance.

Bob Neal's two biggest problems at this time were getting radio stations to play Elvis's records, and toning down the act for small-town clubs. Country stations thought Elvis sounded like a rhythm-and-blues singer, and blues stations found him too country for their listeners. The trio's frenzied performances were considered by many club owners to be too wild. In addition to Elvis's antics, bass player Bill Black liked to clown it up by dancing with his huge bass fiddle and rolling around on the floor. By 1955 these problems had pretty much taken care of themselves. Elvis's sound had become better known through his weekly appearances on the *Louisiana Hayride*, and his new-found fame brought the band bookings in larger towns, where their act was more acceptable. The Hillbilly Cat and the Blue Moon Boys added drummer D.J. Fontana and began to appear with well-established country acts, including the Wilburn Brothers, Faron Young, Ferlin Huskey, Roy Acuff, Kitty Wells, and the Carter Family.

Drummer D.J. Fontana joined Elvis's combo in the early spring of 1955.

During 1955 Sun released three more Elvis singles: "Milkcow Blues Boogie"/"You're a Heartbreaker" in January; "I'm Left, You're Right, She's Gone"/"Baby, Let's Play House" in April; and "Mystery Train"/"I Forgot to Remember to Forget" in August. Like all his early records, these singles have a rhythm-and-blues song on one side and a country tune on the other. Elvis was still considered a regionally based country-western performer, but his popularity was now beginning to soar. "Baby, Let's Play House" was his first record to appear on a national chart: It rose to number ten on the country lists.

Early in his career, Elvis toured with country heartthrob Faron Young.

Elvis backstage with the Wilburn Brothers.

Elvis also appeared onstage with such well-established country acts as Kitty Wells.

Audiences in some of the smaller towns across the South found the Hillbilly Cat and the Blue Moon Boys
too wild for their tastes. In addition to Elvis's show-stopping performance style, Bill Black (right) loved to clown
around with his bass fiddle.

CHAPTER FOUR

CONTRACT WITH THE

COLONEL

I'd rather try and close a deal with

the devil.

HAL WALLIS ON

COLONEL TOM PARKER

In June 1955, Elvis hired Memphis photographer William Speer, who arranged what is probably the most striking and romanticized photo session Elvis ever sat for. This Speer photo captures Elvis's smoldering good looks.

Colonel Tom Parker first saw Elvis Presley in the spring of 1955. Bob Neal had booked the Hillbilly Cat and the Blue Moon Boys on a tour with country singer Hank Snow. The tour was organized by Hank Snow Jamboree Attractions, which was owned by Snow but operated by Colonel Tom Parker, a former carnival barker who had guided Eddy Arnold to stardom. There are lots of stories about Parker; some are no doubt true, while others are probably fabrications. It's said that he once covered a hot plate with straw and set baby chickens on top of it to make them "dance" to the tune "Turkey in the Straw." Another story has Parker painting sparrows yellow and selling them as parakeets. Whatever else anyone has to say about Colonel Tom Parker, everyone agrees that he is a shrewd man.

By mid-1955, Elvis hysteria had begun to set in among teenage girls.

By mid-1955 a large portion of Elvis's audience was made up of teenage girls. They were especially enthusiastic during his stage performances, and Elvis learned to play to the girls in the audience, teasing them with his gyrations and making them scream each time he swiveled his hips. During a summer performance in Jacksonville, Florida, Elvis jokingly invited all the girls in the audience to meet him backstage. But the joke was on Elvis: A swarm of screaming girls chased him all the way to his car and literally ripped off most of his clothes. This event terrified his mother and surprised the press, but it delighted the Colonel, who had begun to monitor Elvis's career closely. Over the next few months Parker watched the steady increase of his popularity.

As with other important events in Elvis's career, there are many versions of the story of how Colonel Tom Parker became Elvis's manager. Parker was supposed to have had a close working relationship with Hank Snow, but when he finally signed Elvis to a contract, Parker did not include Snow in the deal. Parker and Snow broke up their partnership, but Snow did not sue. Some suggest that Snow didn't sue because Parker had something on him; others say that Snow threatened to sue but never got around to following through.

Elvis stepped into the big-time when he signed a contract with RCA Records in late 1955. On hand were (left to right) his new manager Colonel Tom Parker, Parker's former client Eddie Arnold, Elvis, and RCA executive Steve Sholes.

Hot times down South: In the summer of 1955, Elvis's performing style seduced and captivated his primarily Southern audience. Elvis's habit of mauling the microphone sent his fans into a screaming frenzy.

After several incidents in which excited fans tore the clothes from Elvis's body, police protection became a necessary part of performing in concert. Elvis remained nonchalant about the matter. "I don't mind if the fans rip the shirt from my back," he said, "they put it there in the first place."

When the Colonel and Elvis signed their first contract in August 1955, Bob Neal still had a contract as Elvis's personal manager. Parker initially signed on as a special adviser whose specific duties were to "assist in any way possible the buildup of Elvis Presley as an artist." Parker was also given the right to negotiate renewals on all existing contracts. Neal was kept on just as a courtesy, and he had virtually no influence over Elvis. When Neal's contract with Elvis expired on March 15, 1956, he was completely out of the picture, and Parker became Elvis's full-time manager at a 25 percent cut.

In many versions of the Elvis Presley legend, Parker is considered to be a bad guy who controlled Elvis's every move. The people who see Parker in this way sight his background as a carnival hustler, his unsophisticated approach to promotion, and the questionable movie deals he locked Elvis into during the 1960s. In the early 1980s information came to light that furthered this negative depiction of the Colonel. During the course of a lawsuit filed against Parker by Elvis's estate, which stemmed from a court-ordered investigation of Parker's management of Elvis, the Colonel admitted that he was not Thomas Parker of Huntington, West Virginia, but Andreas van Kuijk from Breda, Holland. This information had surfaced earlier, but Parker did not openly admit it until it was to his advantage. Since he was not a United States citizen, he could not be sued under federal law. The case was later settled out of court.

Colonel Parker never missed an opportunity to hawk a few wares to the fans during an Elvis concert.

After Colonel Parker exposed Elvis to a national audience, the controversy surrounding the hot young singer began to flare. Newspapers and magazines attacked Elvis on a number of fronts, including his flashy attire and his long ducktail haircut.

Elvis demonstrates the notorious Presley sneer that so delighted his fans.

All employees at RCA seemed caught up in celebrating Elvis's new contract. In this publicity photo, several hold models of Nipper, the famous RCA mascot.

Elvis's fans and biographers continue to speculate about why he let Colonel Parker have total control of his career. It's been suggested that since Elvis kept himself isolated from people in Hollywood and show business circles, he knew no one who was qualified to advise him on choosing scripts and other material. This would have made it easier for Elvis to accept the Colonel's decisions. It's also been said that Parker was not only greedy, but also had a desperate need for power and controlling Elvis was his way of feeling powerful. The most outrageous hypothesis (put forth by record producer Phil Spector, among others) is that the Colonel controlled Elvis by hypnosis. A "behind-the-scenes" opinion is given by Priscilla Beaulieu Presley in *Elvis and Me*. She says that it was very difficult to make Parker back down. Even though Elvis sometimes complained about the ridiculous songs he was asked to record, he stopped short of refusing to do what the Colonel wanted him to do because he didn't want to risk jeopardizing his extravagant and often excessive lifestyle. Since both Elvis and his father hated the business part of his career and distrusted anyone associated with business, they relied on the Colonel to take care of all the details—from income taxes and investments to contracts and career moves. According to Priscilla, Elvis would sign a contract without even reading it.

Priscilla also wrote that Elvis felt trapped into making musical comedies and that he often hated the soundtrack music. When he talked about *G.I. Blues* with her, Elvis complained that there were too many songs in the movie and that none of them were any good. Elvis wanted to make music his own way, but the Colonel insisted that he always perform as a star. Elvis loved to harmonize with his backup groups, who were often gospel quartets, such as the Jordanaires. Parker objected to this and told Elvis that his fans wanted to hear his voice loud and clear. In one recording session the Colonel even pretended he was letting Elvis sing the way he wanted. But when the album was released, Elvis's voice was emphasized as usual. He suspected that the recording engineers were under orders to tamper with the final version of each song so that his voice would dominate.

Despite Parker's dubious tactics, he was perhaps the single most important force behind Elvis's rise to national stardom. Some people try to discount Parker's contribution to Elvis's career by concentrating on his less-scrupulous dealings or by speculating that Elvis let Parker control him because of something unethical. They even go so far as to say that Elvis would have been a much bigger star if he had not been managed by the Colonel. But these people misunderstand the important role Parker played in Elvis's fame. Parker's master plan for Elvis was a steady pursuit of the big time, gradually encompassing larger and larger audiences in all parts of the country. Parker and everyone in his management team wanted to groom Elvis to become a mainstream entertainer—a movie star and a pop singer. Colonel Parker achieved his goal for Elvis beyond his wildest expectations.

In the late summer of 1955, when Parker began to take part in Elvis's career, Elvis was still just a country singer. His style wasn't traditional, and many of his most loyal fans were teenagers; but he toured the country circuits and performed with well-known country stars, and his records were played almost exclusively on country stations. If Elvis was going to live up to the potential the Colonel saw in him, he would have to be exposed to audiences outside the South.

Elvis's first single release on the RCA label was "Heartbreak Hotel."

Colonel Parker was responsible for some of the most significant moves in Elvis's career.

Elvis is captured on the verge of phenomenal national success.

Parker began his pursuit of the big time for Elvis by negotiating a recording contract with RCA. Other record companies with national distribution, including Columbia and Atlantic, were also interested in Elvis, but Parker had several contacts at RCA that made a deal with that company preferable. Sam Phillips sold Elvis's recording contract to RCA for $35,000 plus $5,000 in royalties. Hill and Range, the music publishers, paid $15,000 of the total amount. RCA acquired all of Elvis's Sun recordings, including the unissued material, and now had the exclusive right to record him. Hill and Range received Hi-Lo Music, the small publishing company owned by Sam Phillips that was responsible for publishing the original material Elvis had recorded at Sun Records.

After the deal was finalized, Hill and Range set up two new music publishing companies: Elvis Presley Music and Gladys Music. These companies would hold the rights to all the songs Elvis recorded. This set-up was financially advantageous for Elvis because he received not only a performer's royalty every time he recorded a song but also a publishing royalty. Hill and Range received half of the income generated by Elvis Presley Music and Gladys Music. The songwriters who published their songs through these two companies gave up a large percentage of their royalties to the music publishers for the opportunity to write songs for Elvis. They were also required to give Elvis a cowriting credit, even though he never wrote a song or any part of a song during his entire career. But the songwriters didn't complain; even with reduced royalties they made a lot of money because every song Elvis recorded sold millions of copies. Although the arrangement was financially beneficial for everyone involved, it limited the number and to some extent the quality of the songs Elvis could record. His contract did not restrict him from recording songs published by other companies, but songwriters who had exclusive agreements with other publishers couldn't write songs for him. From time to time Elvis ended up singing mediocre material written by the hack writers Hill and Range had under contract.

Some people say the quality of Elvis's music began to deteriorate as soon as he started to record for RCA. They lay the blame for this on everything from the tightly structured recording schedule at RCA, which was totally different from the down-home atmosphere at Sun, to Elvis's own desire to sing like Dean Martin. Most people agree that after he went to RCA, Elvis's music was still as good as ever, but his sound did become more mellow than it had been.

While touring Florida in the summer of 1956, the Colonel helped Elvis bargain for a white Lincoln Continental to add to the young singer's ever-growing fleet of fancy cars.

Elvis looked in top form in August 1956, when he performed before record-breaking crowds in Miami, Florida. "I'm not kidding myself," Elvis declared. "My voice alone is just an ordinary voice. What people come to see is how I use it."

Chapter Five

The
Ed Sullivan Show

When I first knew Elvis,

he had a million dollars worth of talent.

Now he has a million dollars.

Colonel Tom Parker

1956

Elvis heeded Colonel Parker's advice on all matters concerning his career.

In the course of a few months in 1956, Elvis Presley left his Southern country roots behind and became a nationally known rock 'n' roll star. The speed of his transition was breathtaking, but it was no accident. Colonel Tom Parker knew what he was doing. But even he couldn't foresee the controversy that would surround Elvis's quick rise to the top. Parker's decision to expose Elvis to a nationwide audience was deliberate. It wasn't a case of being in the right place at the right time, or merely the logical next step in Elvis's career; Parker was taking a carefully calculated risk that happened to pay off. When Parker signed Elvis with RCA, he also used his connections to secure Elvis a contract with the William Morris Agency, a top entertainment-management company. With both RCA and William Morris promoting him, Elvis took the country by storm.

Steve Sholes (left), the head of RCA's country music division, wisely decided to exploit Elvis's attractiveness to the teenage audience rather than market him as a country singer.

The executives at RCA, including Steve Sholes, who was the head of RCA's country music division, immediately realized that Elvis's singing and performing style was different from traditional country musicians. Rather than downplaying these differences, RCA and William Morris decided to exploit them in the hope of building up Elvis's growing teenage audience. By the mid-1950s teenagers had begun to listen almost exclusively to rock 'n' roll, so Elvis was encouraged to turn away from country music and devote himself to a new rock 'n' roll image.

Elvis began the year 1956 as a country singer; he ended it as America's first rock 'n' roll star.

While the desire for the largest possible audience for Elvis was the primary reason for his shift away from country music, there was also another motivation. The powers that be in country music were beginning to resent Elvis and his different style of music. Some of the more traditional country singers didn't want to follow Elvis's high-voltage act when they performed with him, and several Nashville music executives tried to get Elvis removed from *Billboard*'s best-selling country chart because his music sounded too much like rhythm and blues.

In January 1956 Elvis recorded his first hit single for RCA: "Heartbreak Hotel." It was an instant success all over the United States. By April, "Heartbreak Hotel" was number one on many country and pop charts, and it climbed as high as number five on some rhythm-and-blues charts. Unlike the songs Elvis had recorded for Sun Records, "Heartbreak Hotel" was a new tune written especially for him. Mae Axton and Tommy Durden tailored the song's lyrics and its blues-influenced sound and dramatic tone to Elvis's singing style. Only the exaggerated echo on the recording recalls Elvis's earlier Sun

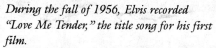

With the help of friend Judy Spreckles, Elvis gets down to the job of answering his voluminous fan mail.

During the fall of 1956, Elvis recorded "Love Me Tender," the title song for his first film.

Elvis discovered that the price of popularity was a sudden lack of privacy. Wherever he went, the young star was mobbed by fans.

53

records. The effective blues piano accompaniment in "Heartbreak Hotel" had not been used before. The loneliness and alienation of "Heartbreak Hotel," coupled with Elvis's emotional interpretation, was aimed directly at his teenage audience, and they loved it.

Elvis's first RCA recording session was a familiar mix of rhythm-and-blues and country songs. In addition to "Heartbreak Hotel," Elvis recorded Ray Charles's tune, "I Got a Woman" (in England it was released on albums as "I Got a Sweetie"), an R&B song, "Money Honey," and two new ballads, "I Was the One" and "I'm Counting on You." (Country singer Kitty Wells turned "I'm Counting on You" into a hit.) The syncopation of the lyrics (the hiccuping sound) on "Money Honey" and the extended guitar solos by Scotty Moore are reminiscent of Elvis's Sun recordings. These recordings also have the same basic instrumentation as Elvis's Sun releases: electric lead guitar, acoustic rhythm guitar, string bass, and drums. But during 1956, as Elvis recorded more material at RCA, he began to move further away from his Sun sound with its country influences, and to move closer to a fully integrated rock 'n' roll style.

When Elvis recorded "Hound Dog" on July 2, 1956, he was going for a big, explosive sound. "Hound Dog" was originally written for blues singer Willa Mae "Big Mama" Thornton, but it had been recorded by many singers since Big Mama's initial release in 1953. Elvis developed his version of the song from a rock 'n' roll arrangement by a group called Freddy Bell and the Bellboys. He'd heard the number in a club in Las Vegas and been impressed by Bell's fast pace and his variations on the lyrics that made them more acceptable to a general audience. Bell also added the famous line, "You ain't never caught a rabbit . . . ." Elvis used Bell's arrangement for his recording of the song. "Hound Dog" was Elvis's longest-running number-one hit in 1956.

"Don't Be Cruel," another hit song that moved Elvis's musical style closer to pure rock 'n' roll, was the flip side of "Hound Dog." This new tune was written by Otis Blackwell in 1955, and Elvis was the first singer to record it. Since it was not associated with any other singer's style or any particular category of music, Elvis could make "Don't Be Cruel" entirely his own. The easygoing but fast-paced rhythm, light tone, and harmonious backup vocals by the Jordanaires show how far removed Elvis was from R&B and country music.

While recording at RCA, Elvis began using the gospel group the Jordanaires for distinctive background vocals.

Elvis and bass player Bill Black pause between takes in the RCA studios.

Elvis often relaxed during recording sessions by playing gospel songs on the piano.

Although Ed Sullivan swore Elvis would never be on his family-oriented variety program, Elvis actually performed on The Ed Sullivan Show *three times in his early career. Here, backed by the Jordanaires, Elvis makes his second appearance, on October 28, 1956.*

Elvis was introduced to the television audience through his six appearances on Stage Show, *hosted by bandleaders Tommy and Jimmy Dorsey.*

On January 28, two weeks after Elvis's first RCA recording session, he made his first television appearance on Tommy and Jimmy Dorsey's weekly variety program, *Stage Show*. Elvis sang "Shake, Rattle and Roll" and "Heartbreak Hotel." During the next eight weeks he appeared on *Stage Show* five more times. Each time he got better ratings. The first show was only moderately successful; *The Perry Como Show* attracted more viewers that night. Elvis was visibly nervous. He sang his two numbers, shook and shimmied a little, and then quickly moved offstage. But by his final appearance, Elvis was going all out to interact with the studio audience. When he strummed the opening chords of "Heartbreak Hotel" on his guitar, a burst of screams and applause broke out. Then Elvis started moving all over the stage, shaking his shoulders, moving his legs, and driving the girls in the audience into a screaming frenzy.

Stage Show always had guest emcees, and on Elvis's first appearance he was introduced by Cleveland disc jockey Bill Randle, who was said to have been the first person outside the South to play one of Elvis's records on the air. On later shows Elvis appeared with entertainers with whom he had no connection at all, including jazz singers Sarah Vaughan and Ella Fitzgerald, stand-up comedians Joe E. Lewis and Henny Youngman, a chimpanzee act called Tippy and Cobina, an acrobatic team known as the Tokayers, and 11-year-old organist Glenn Derringer. Teaming Elvis with these performers called attention to his high-powered music, his wild performing style, and his exaggerated ducktail haircut and Beale Street clothes.

Looking back, it all seems pretty harmless, but Elvis appeared on the scene at a time when rock 'n' roll was coming under fire in the national media. To some people Elvis represented everything that was dangerous about rock music. During the spring and summer of 1956, many national magazines published articles that claimed there was a link between rock 'n' roll and juvenile delinquency. Elvis was sometimes featured in articles that sensationalized the effect of his suggestive performing style on teenage girls. When the press was not openly criticizing Elvis, they were ridiculing him. Despite the fact that his music was identified as rock 'n' roll, journalists and reporters often referred to Elvis as a "hillbilly singer." He was maligned for his Southern accent, his flashy clothes, his long sideburns, and the pomade in his hair.

To many parents, clergy, politicians, and even established show business professionals, Elvis represented everything that was dangerous about rock 'n' roll. Much maligned for his clothes, his hair, his Southern accent, and his uninhibited sexuality, Elvis was viewed by some as a threat to "good taste."

*No longer called the Hillbilly Cat
and the Blue Moon Boys, the
act was referred to as simply "Elvis
Presley" by 1956.*

Between television appearances and recording sessions, Elvis continued to tour

the South and Southwest. Along with Scotty Moore, Bill Black, and D.J. Fontana, he kept

up a breakneck pace. The group was no longer known as the Hillbilly Cat and the Blue

Moon Boys. The act was simply called "Elvis Presley," with no acknowledgement of the

band. In April 1956 the Colonel booked Elvis for a two-week engagement at the New

Frontier Hotel in Las Vegas. The gig turned out to be a disaster. Perhaps Parker should

have known better than to book Elvis into a major engagement outside the South with an

audience made up mostly of adults. After a few performances, Elvis was bumped to

second billing in favor of a more typical Vegas entertainer, comedian Shecky Greene.

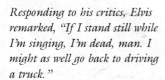

*Responding to his critics, Elvis
remarked, "If I stand still while
I'm singing, I'm dead, man. I
might as well go back to driving
a truck."*

One of the many publicity photos sent to Elvis's fans during the early part of his career.

In April of 1956, Elvis made his Las Vegas debut at the New Frontier Hotel, with disastrous results. Before the engagement was finished, he was reduced to second billing behind comedian Shecky Greene. One reporter cruelly likened Elvis's performance to "a jug of corn liquor at a champagne party."

Elvis in a contemplative mood beside the pool in Las Vegas.

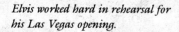

Elvis worked hard in rehearsal for his Las Vegas opening.

Elvis's unsuccessful engagement at the New Frontier can be blamed on the audiences, who were not accustomed to seeing rock 'n' roll singers in Vegas.

The Colonel offers Elvis some advice during rehearsal for his second appearance on The Milton Berle Show. *Costarring on this program was Irish McCalla (seated behind Elvis), who starred on television as Sheena, Queen of the Jungle.*

Elvis and the Jordanaires sing "I Want You, I Need You, I Love You" on The Milton Berle Show.

In the late spring of 1956 Elvis appeared on *The Milton Berle Show* for the first time. In June, when he did Berle's show for the second time, Elvis sang the as-yet-unrecorded "Hound Dog" for the first time on television. His performance fanned the flames of controversy over his hip-swiveling performing style. When he began the song, no one knew what to expect because the tune was new. But the audience immediately responded enthusiastically, and Elvis was inspired to go further. He slowed down the final chorus to a blues tempo and thrust his pelvis to the beat of the music in a particularly suggestive manner. The studio audience went wild. The interaction between Elvis and his audience added to the power of his performance. The smile on his face showed his delight in the explosive effect he had on his fans. The interaction between Elvis and the women in his audiences was already becoming a game: Elvis teased the women with his provocative moves, they screamed for more, he promised to go further, and sometimes he did.

The next day, newspaper critics outdid one another in expressing outrage over Elvis's television performance. At least one writer compared it to a striptease. Jack Gould of the *New York Times* declared, "Mr. Presley has no discernible singing ability," while John Crosby of the *New York Herald Tribune* called Elvis "unspeakably untalented and vulgar." The criticism prompted parents, religious groups, and the Parent-Teacher Association to condemn Elvis.

After Milton Berle's show Colonel Parker booked Elvis on *The Steve Allen Show*, a new variety program that aired at the same time as Ed Sullivan's immensely popular show. Allen hated rock 'n' roll, but he was aware of the high ratings Berle's show had received when Elvis appeared. He was also aware of the controversy. To tone down Elvis's sexy performance, Allen insisted that he wear a tuxedo during his segment, and he introduced him as "the new Elvis Presley." Elvis sang one of his latest singles, a slow but hard-driving ballad called "I Want You, I Need You, I Love You." Immediately after that number, the curtain opened to reveal a cuddly basset hound sitting on a tall wooden stand. Elvis sang "Hound Dog" to the docile creature, who easily upstaged the singer with his sad-eyed expression. Later in the program Elvis joined Steve Allen, Imogene Coca, and fellow Southerner Andy Griffith in a comedy sketch satirizing country radio programs like the *Louisiana Hayride*. Allen used humor to cool down Elvis's sensual performing style, prohibited him from moving around too much on stage and even prevented him from wearing his trademark Beale Street clothes. The fans were furious, and they picketed NBC-TV studios the next morning with placards that read, "We want the gyratin' Elvis." But Steve Allen came out a winner; his show beat Sullivan in the ratings without generating controversy.

Elvis had established himself as an entertainer who could attract a large television audience and boost ratings, so it's not surprising that after many rejections the Colonel finally arranged for Elvis to appear on *The Ed Sullivan Show*, the highest-rated prime-time variety program on the air. Sullivan, who was a powerful figure in the industry, had stated publicly that he would not allow Elvis to appear on his show because it was a family program. But ratings speak louder than scruples, and Sullivan backed down from this stance after *The Steve Allen Show* was so successful. Elvis was paid an unprecedented $50,000 for three appearances on *The Ed Sullivan Show*. This was a lot more than the $5,000 per show Colonel Parker had asked for only a few weeks earlier when Sullivan turned him down.

The first two times Elvis appeared on *The Ed Sullivan Show*, he was not censored. But on his third and final appearance in January 1957, Elvis can be seen only from the waist up while he is singing. The CBS censors would not allow Elvis's entire body to be shown, but despite the censorship, Elvis put on an exciting show. The screams and applause from the studio audience let the television audience know what Elvis was up to on stage, defeating the purpose of the censorship. After Elvis's performance Sullivan declared him to be "a real decent, fine boy."

Elvis is fitted for the tuxedo he would wear during his appearance on The Steve Allen Show.

Steve Allen applauds Elvis's sedate costume during a dress rehearsal.

Elvis appeared with Allen, Andy Griffith (not pictured), and comedienne Imogene Coca in a sketch lampooning country radio programs like Louisiana Hayride.

As "Tumbleweeds Presley" on The Steve Allen Show, *Elvis held up his end of a conventional variety-program comedy sketch.*

Allen softened the sexual overtones of Elvis's rendition of "Hound Dog" by having Elvis sing the tune to a basset hound.

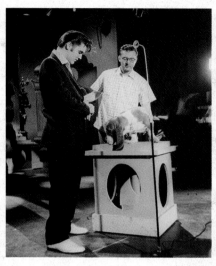

Elvis was a good sport about appearing on The Steve Allen Show with a real hound dog, but years later he would resent being ridiculed by Allen.

Between the basset hound and the tuxedo, Allen succeeded in taming Elvis's act, at least for this program. Elvis's fans, however, were furious and picketed the NBC studios the next day.

Steve Allen introduced Elvis by referring to him as the "new Elvis Presley," after which the controversial young singer appeared in formal attire.

This single appearance on The Milton Berle Show *in June of 1956, during which Elvis sang a provocative version of "Hound Dog," was responsible for the criticism that his performing style was nothing more than a striptease—a comparison that would haunt him for many years.*

Elvis and Ed Sullivan joke during rehearsal before one of Elvis's legendary appearances on The Ed Sullivan Show.

For years people have wondered why Elvis was shown only from the waist up during his third time on Sullivan's show. The simplest explanation is that Sullivan received negative criticism about the earlier appearances. Other explanations include the theory that the Colonel had forced Sullivan to apologize publicly for remarks he'd made about Elvis to the press during the previous summer, and the waist-up-only order was Sullivan's way of getting back at Parker. The wildest explanation was offered by a former director of *The Ed Sullivan Show*, who said that during his second appearance Elvis put a cardboard tube in his trousers and manipulated it to make the studio audience scream. To avoid a repeat performance, Sullivan supposedly insisted on above-the-waist coverage for Elvis's final appearance.

The now-famous Ed Sullivan Show *appearance in which Elvis was shot only from the waist up was actually the young singer's third time on the program.*

*Elvis's hometown of Tupelo, Mississippi, honored its native son with
a proclamation designating September 26, 1956, as Elvis Presley
Day. The celebration took place during the Mississippi-Alabama Fair
and Dairy Show, where a parade and two concerts by Elvis
were highlights. Elvis's guests for the festivities included his parents
as well as Barbara Hearn, one of Elvis's girlfriends. Eleven
years earlier, Elvis had won second prize in the fair's talent show with
his stirring rendition of "Old Shep."*

CHAPTER SIX

ELVIS
GOES TO HOLLYWOOD

When I ran the test I felt the same thrill I experienced

when I first saw Errol Flynn on the screen.

Elvis, in a very different, modern way, had exactly the same power,

virility, and sexual drive.

The camera caressed him.

HAL WALLIS

Film producer Hal Wallis was fascinated by Elvis's instinctual approach to recording. Elvis would record take after take, listen to all of them, and then select the one he felt sounded right.

Actor Robert Wagner, seated next to Elvis in this photo, was considered for Elvis's role in Love Me Tender.

The first time independent movie producer Hal Wallis saw Elvis perform, he was convinced that Elvis was going to become a major star. Wallis was a former executive producer at Warner Brothers and had formed Hal Wallis Productions in 1944. He had been in the movie business for 25 years and had a stellar reputation. In early 1956 Wallis happened to catch Elvis's act on the television variety program *Stage Show*. The electrifying effect Elvis had on the women in the studio audience spelled movie magic to Wallis. Wasting no time, he called Colonel Parker the next morning to set up a screen test for the controversial young singer. Parker probably disguised his eagerness to get Elvis into the movies, and then casually he let Wallis know that Elvis was planning a trip to the West Coast in the near future. Perhaps they could set up a meeting, the wily agent told the eager filmmaker.

On April 1, 1956, Elvis did a screen test with veteran character actor Frank Faylen. They performed a scene from N. Richard Nash's play, *The Rainmaker*, which was soon to be made into a movie. It may have been April Fools' Day, but Elvis's performance was seen as no joke. He was so good that Wallis arranged a three-picture deal with him. If Hal Wallis had confidence in Elvis as an actor, then Hollywood was willing to accept that the young singer was well on his way to becoming a movie star.

Elvis had always loved the movies. When he was in high school, he was an usher at Loew's State Theater in Memphis. Later in his life, when his superstar status prevented him from going out in public, Elvis often rented an entire theater just to watch one movie in peace. From the beginning of his career, Elvis wanted to be a movie actor. When his sudden notoriety opened the door for this to happen, he was eager to do whatever he had to do to make a career in the movies. "Singers come and go," Elvis said, "but if you're a good actor, you can last a long time."

At this time Wallis was working exclusively for Paramount Pictures, but that studio had no suitable script for Elvis when he signed his contract with Wallis. So Elvis was loaned to Twentieth Century Fox for a Civil War drama called *The Reno Brothers*. His part in the movie was a secondary role, and both Robert Wagner and Jeffrey Hunter had originally been considered for the part. It was the first and last movie Elvis appeared in that was not specifically designed as a vehicle for him.

Elvis discovered that his rustic wardrobe for Love Me Tender *was a far cry from the hip Beale Street clothes he usually wore.*

The Colonel stayed on the set during the production of many of Elvis's films to make sure his boy was treated properly.

Elvis patiently posed for test shots for his Love Me Tender *wardrobe. As indicated by the chalkboard that Elvis holds, the film's original title was* The Reno Brothers.

Many of the lobby cards and ads for Love Me Tender *emphasized Elvis, even though he was not the star of this film.*

The makeup man prepares Elvis for his next scene.

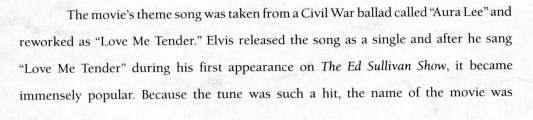

The movie's theme song was taken from a Civil War ballad called "Aura Lee" and reworked as "Love Me Tender." Elvis released the song as a single and after he sang "Love Me Tender" during his first appearance on *The Ed Sullivan Show*, it became immensely popular. Because the tune was such a hit, the name of the movie was

Elvis's fans were shocked and saddened when his character was shot and killed at the end of Love Me Tender.

changed to *Love Me Tender* before it opened in New York on November 15, 1956. The story line follows the fortunes of a farm family after the Civil War. Elvis plays the youngest son, Clint Reno, who marries his eldest brother's girl. Everyone thinks the brother has been killed in the war, but he returns unexpectedly. The family is torn apart by the consequences of the marriage, and in the end Clint is shot and killed.

Exteriors for Love Me Tender *were shot on location in the San Fernando Valley near Los Angeles.*

The producers of *Love Me Tender* worried that Elvis's fans would have a negative reaction to the movie's ending. Elvis's real-life mother, Gladys, was said to be shocked by his on-screen death. No one knew if people would stay away from theaters once word got out that Elvis's character was going to die in the last few frames. In the movie's original ending, Mother Reno, played by Mildred Dunnock, rings the bell for dinner, and the remaining Reno brothers come in to supper. The pain and sadness on their faces indicates that Clint has gone to the Great Beyond. The end credits immediately follow this poignant, downbeat scene. After the shooting of *Love Me Tender* was completed, Elvis was called back to make another ending for the movie in which his character survives. But in the version that was actually released, the movie has a compromise ending. Clint Reno is killed, but Elvis's face is superimposed over the final scene as he sings "Love Me Tender." This version rings true to the original script, but fans are left with a more positive image of their idol.

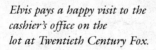

Elvis pays a happy visit to the cashier's office on the lot at Twentieth Century Fox.

No specially catered meals for Elvis—he was content to eat the same simple boxed lunch as other members of the cast and crew.

Love Me Tender has only four musical numbers, but the song "Love Me Tender" was such a big hit for Elvis that no one seemed to notice how few songs were in the movie. Some people claim that Hal Wallis let it be known that Elvis's faithful backup musicians, Scotty Moore, Bill Black, and D.J. Fontana, were not welcome in Hollywood. Supposedly he thought they were too unsophisticated to participate in a Hollywood recording session. A group called the Ken Darby Trio backed up Elvis in the soundtrack recording sessions, but this was not Wallis's choice. He had nothing to do with the production of *Love Me Tender* because it was released by Twentieth Century Fox. The story about the musicians is either untrue or it is about another producer. In fact, Moore, Black, and Fontana appear in several movies Elvis later made for Wallis.

Although Love Me Tender *was set in the 1800s, Elvis's rendition of the musical numbers was quite modern.*
Here costars Richard Egan and Mildred Dunnock enjoy Elvis's rocking version of "We're Gonna Move."

The star of Love Me Tender, *Richard Egan, genuinely liked Elvis and helped him through several of his scenes. Years later their paths would cross again. During Elvis's February 1972 engagement in Las Vegas, Egan stood up and began an ovation for Elvis after the final number.*

76

Elvis probably had a crush on costar Debra Paget, but her mother (seated above) had other plans for her daughter, which didn't include romance.

Elvis seems to have gotten along well with his costars, and he often deferred to their greater experience in making movies. Richard Egan, who played elder brother Vance Reno, said about Elvis: "That boy could charm the birds from the trees. He was so eager and humble, we went out of our way to help him." Throughout the making of the movie, Elvis may have nursed a crush on costar Debra Paget, beginning a career-long habit of falling for his female costars. But Debra probably just ignored his attentions. She was a few years older than Elvis and dedicated to her career. Her mother, who was often on the set, had big plans for Debra, none of which involved Elvis.

As the huge cut-out of Elvis was unveiled, deafening screams could be heard from the crowd below.

Fans descend on the Paramount Theater in New York for the unveiling of a 40-foot cut-out of Elvis atop the theater's marquee. Notice that some of the signs indicate the fans' displeasure at having their idol killed off in the film.

It's been rumored that Colonel Parker was responsible for printing and distributing the placards carried by the fans during this publicity stunt.

The reviews of Elvis's first big-screen performance were brutal. But that must have come as no surprise since the press had been on his case long before Elvis took up acting. A reporter for *Time* magazine said that Elvis had the screen presence of a sausage. A review in *Variety* was more to the point: "Appraising Presley as an actor, he ain't. Not that it makes any difference." But the critics' sarcasm fell on deaf ears. When a huge cut-out of Elvis as Clint Reno was unveiled on top of New York City's Paramount Theater to promote the movie, thousands of fans showed up to see Elvis larger than life.

The first movie Elvis made for Hal Wallis was *Loving You*. It was developed by Wallis and writer/director Hal Kanter specifically for the young star. This musical drama was designed to showcase Elvis's best talents, and the story line was ingeniously based on Elvis's own life. *Loving You*, which was released by Paramount in July 1957, stars Elvis as an unknown but talented singer who has a totally new sound. His character, Deke

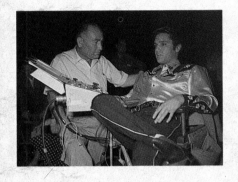

Producer Hal Wallis chats with his young star between takes during the production of Loving You.

The story line of Loving You *closely parallels Elvis's own life. Here Elvis's character, Deke Rivers, sings his heart out on national television.*

Rivers, is from the South, but he doesn't fit in with the country music crowd. A ruthless music promoter, played by Lizabeth Scott, recognizes Deke's unique talent and exploits him as a fresh face who appeals to teenage audiences. The media misrepresents his appeal and brands him a dangerous hothead until Deke proves he has simply been misunderstood. The story line and the well-written tunes tailored to Elvis's musical style were guaranteed to attract his fans. Contrary to popular belief, Elvis received his first on-screen kiss in *Loving You*, not in *Love Me Tender*. The honor went to a young actress named Jana Lund. She had a small role in the movie as a sexy young fan of Deke Rivers.

Costar Dolores Hart played the classic good girl in Loving You. *She later gave up her film career and became a Roman Catholic nun.*

Actress Jana Lund, playing an ardent fan, gave Elvis his first screen kiss.

After a local boy taunts, "Hey, sideburns, why don't you sing us a tune," Elvis's character cuts loose with "Mean Woman Blues."

Elvis chats with his parents, who were part of the audience during the final production number of Loving You.

(From left to right) Wendell Corey, Elvis, Dolores Hart, and Lizabeth Scott headed the cast of Loving You.

Many of Elvis's friends had bit parts in this colorful musical. His guitarist, Scotty Moore, is seated on the far right of this scene, while his drummer, D.J. Fontana, is seated on the far left with his back to the camera.

Wallis wanted the movie to present an accurate view of the music world, so he sent director Hal Kanter to Memphis to observe Elvis's act and the way he lived while he was on the road. Kanter was in Shreveport when Elvis gave one of his last performances on *Louisiana Hayride*. Kanter's movie attempts to capture the excitement Elvis generated in his audience during a concert. The performance scenes in *Loving You* are accurate down to the constant popping of flashbulbs, the hysterical screaming of the audience, and the almost unbearable tension that builds up before Elvis comes on stage. In an article Kanter later wrote for *Variety*, he referred to Elvis's position in this mass hysteria as "the eye of the hurricane." It was a position Elvis would try to maintain for the rest of his life.

Elvis did not date either of his costars, Dolores Hart or Lizbeth Scott, while making *Loving You*. But he did go out with an actress who had a bit part in the movie, Yvonne Lime. She later appeared as a regular on several television shows, including *Father Knows Best* and *The Many Loves of Dobie Gillis*. Yvonne revealed what it was "really" like to date Elvis in the movie magazine *Modern Screen*. The article was just a publicity piece that attempted to present Elvis as a shining example of wholesome living. According to Yvonne, Elvis was a perfect gentleman; he was devoted to his mother and liked to sing religious songs at parties. His rock 'n' roll image, long hair, and sideburns were explained in the article as nothing more than a case of nonconformity. Or as Yvonne would have it, Elvis wore long hair and sideburns for the same reason that adults grow beards.

This costume from Loving You *has become famous among fans because Elvis sang the popular tune "Teddy Bear" while wearing it.*

During the production of Loving You, *Elvis dated starlet Yvonne Lime, who had a small role in the movie.*

Elvis asked Vernon and Gladys to join him in Hollywood for the filming of *Loving You* because he had missed their company so much while making *Love Me Tender*. Hal Kanter arranged for Vernon and Gladys, along with some family friends, to make cameo appearances near the end of the movie as members of a concert audience. After Gladys's death, Elvis refused to watch *Loving You* because it was such a painful reminder of his mother. In addition to his parents, Elvis's longtime backup musicians, Scotty Moore, Bill Black, and D.J. Fontana, also appear in the movie as members of a country band. Even the Jordanaires, the vocal group that frequently sang background harmonies for Elvis, pop up in the movie for a brief appearance.

The soundtrack album for *Loving You*, which was Elvis's third long-playing record for RCA, reached number one on some pop charts. This was the first of Elvis's albums to combine songs from a movie with tracks from recording sessions. These so-called soundtrack albums were released at about the same time as Elvis's movies so that each one promoted the other for the maximum exposure of both.

Elvis's third feature film, *Jailhouse Rock*, opened the same day the title song reached number one. This movie was not made by Hal Wallis's production company: Elvis was loaned to MGM to make this musical drama. While *Loving You* is a polished feature film with showy production numbers, shot in vivid Technicolor, *Jailhouse Rock* is a low-budget, straightforward black-and-white movie with simple back-lot sets and no large-scale production numbers. Far from bringing the movie down, these features enhance the gritty subject matter. *Jailhouse Rock* is generally regarded as the best movie Elvis ever made. Even people who aren't his fans like this movie. *Jailhouse Rock* was not only a critical success, it also made Elvis a lot of money. He received $250,000 for his work on the movie, plus a percentage of the net profits, and he held the publishing rights to all the songs.

Elvis personally choreographed the memorable "Jailhouse Rock" production number.

"Don't you be no square...." Elvis invites everyone to dance to the "Jailhouse Rock."

Fight! Jailhouse Rock *exploited the brooding, hot-blooded side of Elvis's image.*

Elvis stars as Vince Everett, a hotheaded young man who is bitter because he was sent to prison on a manslaughter charge. While he's in the pen, Vince learns to sing and play the guitar from another inmate who had once been a country-western star. After his release from prison, Vince becomes a popular singer whose fresh sound creates a stir in the recording industry. With the help of a record promoter named Peggy Van Alden, who also falls in love with him, Vince enjoys popular success and critical acclaim. The plot echoes Elvis's own career, particularly when Vince is called to Hollywood because of his success as a singer.

Jennifer Holden and Judy Tyler clown around with Elvis outside the stars' dressing rooms.

Elvis's pets in Jailhouse Rock *are cute reminders of his most famous hit record, "Hound Dog."*

Mickey Shaughnessy played Hunk Houghton, the washed-up country singer who teaches his young protégé how to sing and play the guitar.

Unlike *Loving You*, the movie *Jailhouse Rock* plays on the notorious side of Elvis's image: In this movie he's a rebel. Elvis's character is not always likable. His bitterness over his unfair jail sentence is presented as a flaw in his character, but it also allows a brooding, hot-blooded Elvis to explode on the screen. Not surprisingly, by the end of the movie, Vince has reformed into a nice guy who humbly wins the affections of Peggy Van Alden. But before he calms down, the audience is treated to several passionate scenes with provocative and often hip dialogue. During an argument with Peggy, Vince grabs her and kisses her long and hard on the lips. Peggy acts as though she were appalled

Jennifer Holden claims to come "all unglued" during her love scene with Elvis.

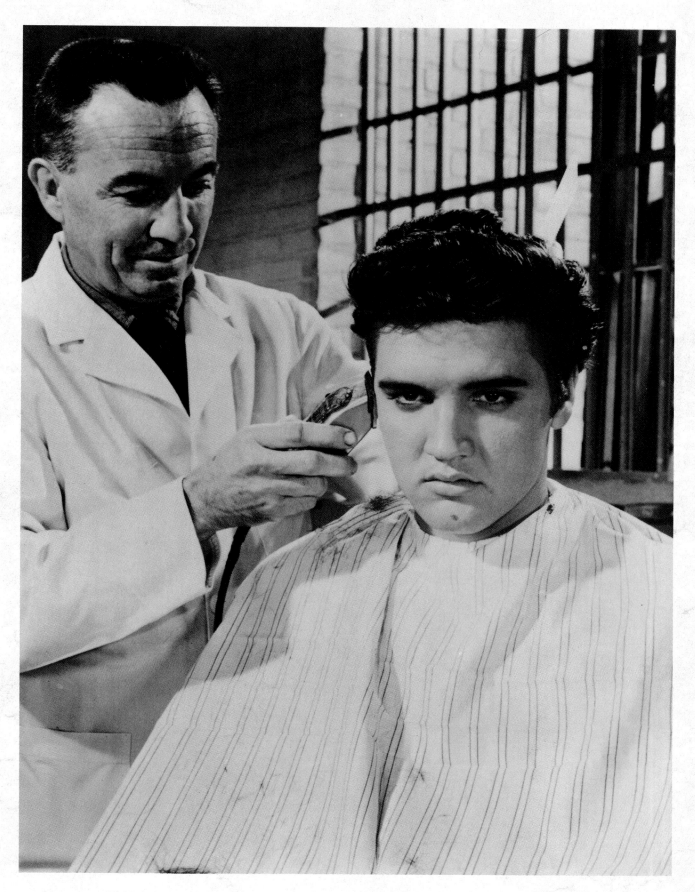

Elvis's fans were shocked to see their idol get his famous ducktail clipped during the prison sequence of Jailhouse Rock. *Some people insist Elvis wore a wig during the haircut scene.*

and haughtily informs Vince that she doesn't appreciate his tactics. Vince coolly replies, "Them ain't tactics, honey; it's just the beast in me." This line supposedly caused many women in movie audiences to fall into full-fledged swoons. In another scene, a Hollywood starlet asks Vince what he thinks of her skimpy outfit. Vince's snappy comeback, "Flippy, really flippy," echoed the ultra-hip slang of a new generation.

Life in Hollywood: "Flippy, really flippy."

Jailhouse Rock also contains several legendary production numbers. The title number was choreographed by Elvis himself. It showcases Elvis's offbeat performing style, using a Hollywood musical format with background dancers and a stylized set. Elvis doesn't cut loose into his notorious gyrations during "Jailhouse Rock," but this musical sequence captures the essence of his off-screen image. Elvis also sings "Baby, I Don't Care" at a Hollywood pool party. All the partygoers are dressed in fashionable, light-colored swimwear except Elvis, who's dressed in black slacks and a black, long-sleeved sweater. Ironically, it is the partygoers who look out of place; Elvis looks hip, not just because of his clothes, but because of his attitude.

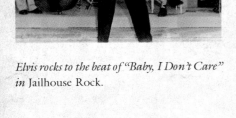

Elvis rocks to the beat of "Baby, I Don't Care" in Jailhouse Rock.

Elvis didn't date his leading lady, Judy Tyler, but he went out occasionally with Anne Neyland, who had a secondary role. Tyler, who plays Peggy Van Alden, had been a regular on the early-1950s children's television show "Howdy Doody." (She was Princess Summerfall Winterspring.) Sadly, Tyler was killed in an auto accident after the principle filming was completed. Her death made it difficult for Elvis to watch *Jailhouse Rock*. He did not attend the movie's preview in Hollywood, and he didn't appear at the premiere in Memphis in the fall of 1957.

Elvis's next movie, *King Creole*, was produced by Hal Wallis for Paramount. This musical drama was based on Harold Robbins's novel, *A Stone for Danny Fisher*. Elvis plays a troubled teenager named Danny Fisher. Dean Jagger costars as Danny's father, a man who has fallen apart emotionally since the death of his wife, letting his family slip into dire poverty. Determined to help his family regain the security and status they once had, Danny quits school to earn money by sweeping floors in a nightclub. A local mobster, played by Walter Matthau, takes an interest in Danny after he hears the talented young man sing. Danny becomes a regular performer in Matthau's club, packing in the crowds with his explosive performing style. But Danny seals his tragic fate when he becomes romantically involved with the club owner's girl.

This ad was part of RCA's promotion for the King Creole *extended-play album.*

As Danny Fisher, Elvis performed in the King Creole nightclub with exotic dancer Forty Nina (Liliane Montevecchi), whose specialty was the song "Banana."

(From left to right) Veteran director Michael Curtiz, producer Hal Wallis, and Elvis discuss an upcoming scene in King Creole.

Wallis purchased *A Stone for Danny Fisher* in 1955, when a play based on the novel was running off-Broadway. Wallis may have originally intended Elvis's part to go to Ben Gazzara, in a movie that would have followed the plot of the novel more closely. James Dean had also been mentioned as a possibility for the role. When Wallis decided to use Elvis for the part of Danny Fisher, the original story line had to be changed to accommodate Elvis's rock 'n' roll image. The setting was changed from New York City to New Orleans, but few characters other than Elvis speak with Southern accents. In the novel Danny is an aspiring boxer; in the movie he's an exciting young singer with a new sound.

Both Wallis and Paramount considered this movie to be an important project. The supporting cast is made up of many notable actors, including Carolyn Jones, Dean Jagger, and Walter Matthau. The movie was directed by well-respected veteran Michael Curtiz, who made *Casablanca*, *Yankee Doodle Dandy*, *Angels with Dirty Faces*, and many other Hollywood classics. The high-quality cast, crew, and locations paid off, and the movie earned Elvis the best movie reviews of his career. Many critics agreed that Elvis had improved tremendously as an actor, while others took note that he was "no longer depicted as the churlish, egotistical singing idol."

King Creole was shot partly on location in New Orleans. There are scenes in the French Quarter, at Lake Pontchartrain, and in an area high school. During location shooting Elvis had a major problem with fans mobbing him at the Roosevelt Hotel, where he was staying. Hal Wallis arranged for heavy-duty security so that Elvis could get enough rest to look fresh on camera. Pinkerton guards patrolled the hallways, the elevators, and even the fire escapes of the hotel to keep well-intentioned but troublesome fans away. When he returned to his hotel in the evening, Elvis had to go up to the top of an adjacent building, cross over the roof, and enter the Roosevelt by way of a fire escape. He was unable to enjoy New Orleans' celebrated nightclubs and famous restaurants because of the persistence of his fans. Shooting in the city streets was even worse, and policemen had to be used for crowd control. During this time in New Orleans, Elvis began to live in seclusion. He had achieved such a high level of popularity that he was forced to stay away from the fans who not only made him a star but also made him a recluse.

Elvis and Carolyn Jones prepare to shoot a scene on location at Lake Pontchartrain. These photos reveal the amount of preparation involved in filmmaking. Although it's only a few minutes long, the scene took several days to shoot.

Carolyn Jones costarred in King Creole as Ronnie, a classic bad girl with a heart of gold.

Elvis's first four movies were nothing like his later musical comedies. Aside from *Love Me Tender*, the plots of his early movies play off aspects of Elvis's image and actual events in his life. *Loving You* is a conventional Hollywood treatment of Elvis's rise to fame; *Jailhouse Rock* capitalized on Elvis's sensual, bad-boy image; and *King Creole* made use of certain details that parallel Elvis's own life. In these movies Elvis was clearly being groomed to take over for actor James Dean, who died in September 1955. Elvis appealed to teenage audiences in much the same way Dean had. An article in *Photoplay* magazine that was published during the shooting of *Love Me Tender* indicated that David Weisbart, the producer of Dean's best-known movie, *Rebel Without a Cause*, was talking to Elvis about portraying Dean in a movie biography. (Elvis's role in *King Creole* had supposedly been offered to Dean.) A special single-issue magazine called *Elvis and Jimmy* from 1956 shows how closely the two young men were linked in the popular imagination. The magazine designated Elvis as the one to take up the fallen hero's leather jacket and become the premier teen rebel.

That Elvis was being groomed to fill the void left by teen hero James Dean is apparent in publicity shots such as this one.

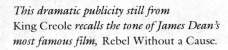

This dramatic publicity still from King Creole *recalls the tone of James Dean's most famous film,* Rebel Without a Cause.

Elvis was a great admirer of James Dean and had memorized the dialogue to Rebel Without a Cause.

Elvis admired James Dean a great deal and must have been flattered by being compared with his hero. *Rebel Without a Cause* was one of Elvis's favorite movies. He memorized all the dialogue and recited Dean's lines whenever he got the chance. When Elvis went to Hollywood, he must have been eager to fill Dean's shoes, but he was humble: "I would never compare myself in any way to James Dean because James Dean was a genius. I sure would like to, I mean, I guess a lot of actors in Hollywood would like to have had the ability that James Dean had, but I would never compare myself to James Dean in any way." For a while Elvis hung out with Dean's crowd, especially the young actor Nick Adams, and he dated Dean's *Rebel* costar, Natalie Wood.

Elvis's link with Dean in the popular imagination was made stronger when Elvis began to pal around with Dean's friends. He and Nick Adams (left) rode bikes together, and Elvis dated Natalie Wood (right).

If Elvis had not gone into the army and come home with a new image, he might have been the new James Dean or become a movie star with a career similar to Frank Sinatra or Bing Crosby. Elvis had been considered for parts in such dramatic features as *The Rainmaker* and *The Defiant Ones*. He was also asked to appear in the musical comedy *The Girl Can't Help It*, starring actress Jayne Mansfield. The movie was to feature the hottest rock 'n' roll stars of the day singing their biggest hits. Little Richard, Gene Vincent, and Eddie Cochran appear in the movie, but the Colonel told the producers that Elvis's fee would be a flat $50,000 for one song. A story reported in Walter Scott's column at the time maintained that Mansfield herself went on a campaign to get Elvis for a more reasonable fee. She flew to Memphis to negotiate with him personally, thinking she could simply end run the Colonel. After spending several days alone with Elvis, Mansfield called Parker and told him that she and Elvis had worked everything out. The Colonel allowed that whatever had happened between them was fine with him, but Elvis's fee was still $50,000 for one song. Later Mansfield told Walter Scott, "I felt somehow that I'd been had."

CHAPTER SEVEN

THIS IS THE ARMY

Elvis died when he went into

the army.

JOHN LENNON

Elvis in his office behind Graceland in December of 1957, the month he received his draft notice.

By 1957 Elvis Presley's image was fully established. He was a notorious rock 'n' roller with a snarl on his lips and too much movement in his hips. His hair and clothing were considered tasteless and sometimes even vulgar. But his most alarming aspect was the effect he had on female audiences: Women screamed uncontrollably throughout most of his performances. Music and movie critics, parents, teachers, community leaders, religious groups, and everyone else who didn't like what they saw in Elvis felt that he inspired chaos and caused young women to become hysterical. Actually, Elvis controlled his audiences masterfully, manipulating their expectations and orchestrating their screaming for maximum effect. Rudy Vallee and Frank Sinatra had a similar effect on their audiences, but the obvious sensuality of Elvis's performing style made him seem more dangerous.

Elvis's movies recast his image somewhat by presenting him as an electrifying talent who had simply been misunderstood by the establishment, but the press continued to criticize him at every turn. Writers for national magazines reinforced the notorious side of his image by harping on the antics of his fans, his greasy hair and sideburns, and his Beale Street attire. Elvis's clothes were a big issue in the press. In 1956 his black slacks with a pink stripe running down the outside of the leg were sighted as being particularly tasteless. But in 1957 Elvis's gold lamé suit drove reporters wild. Elvis had asked famed Hollywood clothing designer Nudie Cohen to create a special gold suit for him for his spring tour. The outfit became known as the "gold tuxedo." Wherever Elvis went, the newspapers never failed to mention the legendary suit, and as the tour progressed, the cost of the suit was reported as being higher and higher. According to the *St. Louis Post-Dispatch*, the suit cost $2,500; the *Fort Wayne News Sentinel* reported that the jacket alone had cost $2,000; and by the time he reached Canada, the price of the suit had gone up to $4,000. Other entertainers, particularly Liberace, could wear outrageous costumes without criticism, but Elvis was ridiculed.

Elvis in 1957: The boy with the snarl on his lips and the moves in his hips.

Elvis was never allowed to do what other entertainers did without being attacked. Even his 1957 Christmas album created a furor. It was a standard Christmas album with fairly conventional arrangements of the usual carols. But a radio station in Portland, Oregon, fired one of its disc jockeys for playing Elvis's "White Christmas" on the air. Dick Whittinghill of station KMPC in Los Angeles refused to play any songs from

The sheer audacity of Elvis's decision to wear a gold lamé suit on his 1957 tour infuriated members of the press, many of whom were already hostile toward the young singer.

The creator of the famous gold suit, Nudie Cohen, poses with Elvis.

A pair of beauty queens, Miss Ohio (left) and Miss Austria (right), point to Elvis's new induction date after he received a draft delay so he could complete King Creole.

Elvis often ventured out to talk to the fans who began gathering around his house in Memphis on a daily basis.

the album. He said that Elvis singing Christmas songs was "like having Tempest Storm [a stripper] give Christmas presents to [his] kids." Several radio stations in Canada banned the album, and Chicago station WCFL banned all of Elvis's records.

The controversy generated by Elvis's image did nothing to deter the adulation of his teenage fans. But their outrageous loyalty did nothing to improve Elvis's relationship with the public as a whole. In 1956 Elvis said: "Teenagers are my life and my triumph. I'd be nowhere without them." But even he could not believe the lengths teens would go to just to be near him. In Texas his fans broke through the plate-glass door of a theater to get close to him. In New Orleans a group of girls tied up an elevator operator, captured Elvis, and held him prisoner inside the elevator. If his fans discovered Elvis's car in a parking lot during or after a concert, they would cover it with messages in lipstick. Fans once broke into his Cadillac and stole his collection of cigarette lighters. They would also cover the exterior of the car with phone numbers scratched into the paint with nail files and jewelry. Rumors circulated that fans were willing to have any body part autographed, and fan magazines warned girls to beware of Elvis's "doll-point pen." Some girls had their hair cut to look like Elvis's famous ducktail, complete with simulated sideburns.

In Memphis fans often hung around his house. Sometimes he would venture outside and talk with them for hours at a time, and Gladys would occasionally serve them refreshments on the patio. Initiates of the Elvis Presley Fan Club were often seen picking blades of grass from the lawn as part of the requirements for membership. The Presleys' neighbors on Audubon Drive brought a suit against them for creating a public nuisance, but the magistrate ruled in favor of Elvis and his family. He maintained that the behavior of his fans was neither Elvis's fault nor his responsibility.

Both Elvis and Colonel Parker wanted to expand his audience to the fullest extent possible. To do this, they knew he would have to change his image. Even before Elvis went into the army, a new kind of publicity began to emerge slowly but surely. A new Elvis Presley, sometimes called the "other Elvis" or the "good Elvis," was in the making. He was to be very different from the dangerous rebel who had caused so much controversy.

The "other Elvis" surfaced for the first time on July 1, 1956, on the television interview program *Hy Gardner Calling*. During the show, syndicated columnist Hy Gardner would call celebrities on the telephone. A split-screen technique allowed viewers to watch both Gardner and the celebrity talking on the phone. The program gave Elvis an opportunity to dispel some of the vicious rumors that were currently circulating about him. He denied that he smoked marijuana to reach a frenetic state for his performances, and he declared that he had never shot at his mother. Viewers saw a down-to-earth Elvis, who admitted that he was confused by his success and said he couldn't see how his critics could think his music was a negative influence on anyone.

Two fans display some of the Elvis Presley merchandise available by late 1956.

Stories about Elvis's close relationship with his parents began to appear in print. The fact that he didn't smoke or drink was brought out in many articles. Elvis was known to be polite during interviews, and he always said "Sir" or "Ma'am" to anyone older than himself. Colonel Parker publicized Elvis's strong feelings about helping less-fortunate people, and booked him for many benefits for charities like the American Cancer Society and the March of Dimes.

Parker also tried to make Elvis seem more wholesome by getting his name and picture on a line of children's products. The Colonel made a deal with promoter Hank Saperstein to merchandise Elvis in much the same way as his other famous clients, including Wyatt Earp, the Lone Ranger, and Lassie, who appeared on everything from lunchboxes to T-shirts. In addition to the usual line of children's items, girls could buy Elvis Presley lipstick in colors like Hound Dog Orange, Tutti Frutti Red, and Heartbreak Hotel Pink. They could also hope for good luck from their Elvis Presley charm bracelets.

Elvis took his pre-induction mental exam for the army in January 1957 and was inducted in March 1958.

Nothing the Colonel or Elvis did to improve his image came close to generating the amount of positive publicity as his induction into the army. Elvis had known for several months that he could be called at any time, and near the end of December 1957, he received his draft notice. Paramount, Elvis, and Hal Wallis requested a two-month deferment from the proposed January induction so that Elvis could finish shooting *King Creole*.

Elvis and other draftees were sworn into the United States Army in Memphis. At the Colonel's invitation, the media photographed and documented each step of the induction process.

On March 24, 1958, Elvis was inducted into the U.S. Army at Fort Chaffee, Arkansas, where his long ducktail haircut was sheared off. He was later transferred to Fort Hood, Texas, for basic training. Elvis refused to join the Army Special Services as an entertainer, and he had turned down enlistment offers from the Marines and the Navy before he was drafted. Elvis's refusal to accept special consideration was seen by the public as admirable, particularly after Colonel Parker leaked to the press exactly how much money Elvis stood to lose by serving his country. Elvis wanted to be treated just like any other G.I., and he always insisted that once his fellow soldiers realized he was there to pull his own weight, they treated him like everyone else.

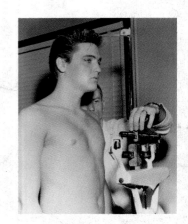

Elvis was concerned about measuring up to Uncle Sam's expectations as well as those of his fellow soldiers.

Gladys and Vernon were at the induction center to say good-bye to their famous son.

Elvis ran his comb through his hair one last time before it was clipped by the army barber.

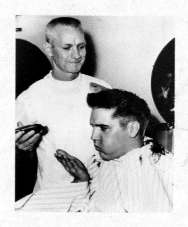

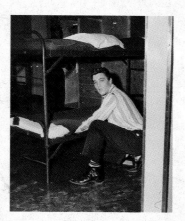

The barber showed no mercy to the most famous locks in show business.

Elvis took the whole thing with his customary sense of humor.

At Ft. Chaffee, Arkansas, Elvis practiced making up his bunk before being issued his fatigues.

Elvis good-naturedly complied with the photographers' request for a salute after reaching Ft. Hood, Texas.

After basic training at Fort Hood Elvis served two years in the Third Armored Division in West Germany. Although he was away from his fans and career, Elvis was not totally absent from the music scene. Parker and RCA had made sure Elvis recorded enough material so that several singles and albums could be released while he was in the army. The movie *King Creole* did not open until several months after his induction, helping to keep Elvis before the public eye.

At Ft. Hood, Elvis was treated no differently than the other young recruits.

Although the army served no peanut-butter-and-banana sandwiches, Elvis never complained about the food.

In this family photo, one of the last taken of Elvis with his parents, Gladys's sorrow is apparent.

Five months after going into the army, Elvis suffered the tragedy of his mother's death. Gladys Presley died on August 14, 1958, possibly from a heart attack related to the acute hepatitis that had hospitalized her. Gladys died at age 46, although many accounts give her age at death as 42. (Gladys was embarrassed to be older than Vernon and often claimed to be four years younger than she actually was.) Elvis was devastated by his mother's death and broke down in front of reporters many times during the days before her funeral. The Blackwood Brothers gospel group sang Gladys's favorite hymns at the funeral, and many celebrities sent condolences, including Marlon Brando, Dean Martin, Ricky Nelson, Tennessee Ernie Ford, and Sammy Davis Jr. Gladys was originally buried at Forest Hill Cemetery in Memphis, but after Elvis died, her remains were moved next to his in Meditation Gardens behind Graceland.

Even at a time of mourning, the photographers would not leave the Presleys alone. Elvis later regretted the media circus that surrounded his mother's funeral.

Gladys was distraught at Elvis's induction into the army, a factor that many claim contributed to her premature death.

Elvis returned to Memphis on emergency leave just in time to visit Gladys before she died on August 14, 1958.

Gladys was originally buried at Forest Hill Cemetery in Memphis, but her body was moved to Meditation Gardens behind Graceland after Elvis died.

SUNSHINE OF OUR HOME
GLADYS LOVE PRESLEY
APR. 25, 1912 — AUG. 14, 1958

NOT MINE
BUT THY WILL BE DONE

Just as American fans gathered outside Elvis's home in Memphis, German followers held vigil outside his house in Bad Nauheim.

Army regulations allowed any soldier who was the sole support of his family to live off the base when he was not on duty. Elvis and his family lived in this house in Bad Nauheim while he was stationed there.

Elvis often invited his fellow soldiers to his house, where the group would sit around the piano and sing, or listen to Elvis sing.

Shortly after his mother's funeral, Elvis was stationed in Bad Nauheim, West Germany, where he was allowed to live in a rented house near the base. He was soon joined by his father, his grandmother, and a few friends. Elvis's German fans were as eager and persistent as his American fans. The Germans called Elvis their "rock 'n' roll matador." In Europe the constant presence of fans and photographers made it difficult for Elvis to enjoy being a tourist.

Even on maneuvers, Elvis would be greeted by fans of all ages.

Elvis dated a Frankfurt girl, Margit Buergin, a few times while stationed in West Germany.

While in the army, Elvis learned that his fans from all over the world were steadfastly loyal.

Near the end of his tour of duty, Presley met 14-year-old Priscilla Beaulieu through a mutual friend, U.S. Airman Currie Grant. She was in West Germany because her stepfather, Air Force Captain Joseph Paul Beaulieu, was stationed in Wiesbaden. Priscilla's father had been killed in a plane crash when she was six months old, and Beaulieu adopted her shortly after he married her mother. Priscilla always referred to him simply as her father. Elvis had been stationed in West Germany for some time before the Beaulieu family arrived, and a story circulates that when Priscilla told her dad that she hoped she'd run into Elvis, he told her that he wouldn't let her walk across the street to see Elvis Presley.

Elvis and Priscilla dated frequently during his last few months in West Germany, but their dates were restricted to her visiting his rented home because of Elvis's inability to go out in public. Elvis enjoyed having a lot of people around when he was home, so it's likely that when Priscilla visited him, several family members and friends were on hand as well. Although she was photographed by the press at the airport when Elvis left for America, there was surprisingly little publicity about Elvis's interest in such a young girl.

Young Priscilla Beaulieu waved good-bye to Elvis as he boarded his flight to the States.

The Colonel and Elvis greeted his fans and the press after a triumphant homecoming from the army in 1960.

Elvis wore his sergeant's stripes proudly. After Elvis's discharge, the Colonel often exaggerated how many stripes his boy had actually earned.

Elvis enjoyed the luxury of a private railroad car for his trip home to Memphis. Unfortunately, the Colonel had filled it with reporters.

103

Elvis met the media several times after his discharge, first in West Germany, then at Ft. Dix, New Jersey, and finally in Memphis.

Concerned that his career might have come to a standstill while in the army, Elvis was relieved to finally be discharged.

Elvis fended off questions about Priscilla, who had been photographed saying good-bye to the rock idol in Germany.

Nancy Sinatra was on hand at the Ft. Dix press conference to present Elvis with a gift from her famous father.

When he got back to the states, Elvis downplayed questions about the girl he left behind. He may have done this to protect the Beaulieus from the press. Almost as soon as Elvis arrived home, gossip columnists began to link him romantically with Frank Sinatra's daughter, Nancy, although the relationship was probably not very significant for either of them.

Priscilla visited Graceland many times over the next couple of years before Elvis finally asked her parents if they would let her stay in Memphis. In 1962 Elvis finally persuaded the Beaulieus to allow Priscilla to live with Vernon and finish school in

Memphis. The press would have had a field day if this information had leaked out, but despite the fact that Priscilla lived with Vernon and his second wife during much of the time she was in high school, Elvis's private life remained private.

Elvis wasn't the only member of the Presley family to find romance in Germany. Vernon also met Dee Stanley (who was then in the process of divorcing her husband) during his son's tour of duty. In July 1960, shortly after Elvis's return to the States, Vernon and Dee were married in Huntsville, Alabama. Some people say that Vernon's second marriage caused friction between Elvis and his father, but it's impossible to say how much it affected their long-term relationship. At any rate, Elvis did not attend his father's wedding ceremony. Ironically, Vernon and Dee's marriage was to end in divorce in 1977, the year Elvis died.

Vernon Presley found romance in Germany when he met Dee Stanley, whom he married in 1960.

While Elvis was in the service, critics speculated that two years away from the public would seriously damage his career and that his position at the forefront of rock 'n' roll would be lost. To some extent they were correct. Elvis didn't return to the vanguard of rock music when he came back from the army. He didn't want to. Elvis and Colonel Parker were no longer interested in rock 'n' roll, which had undergone many changes between 1958 and 1960. Rock musicians were more controversial than ever: Little Richard was in trouble with the IRS; Chuck Berry had been arrested for violating the Mann Act; and Jerry Lee Lewis was ostracized for marrying his 13-year-old cousin when he was already married. While scandal claimed some rockers, others like Buddy Holly had died, and ballad singers were quickly replacing more frenzied rock 'n' roll performers on the charts.

When Elvis returned home in 1960, the stage was set for him to take up a more mellow style. The Colonel took advantage of the good publicity from Elvis's tour of duty to promote a more mature Elvis, whom he hoped would attract a larger audience. The change in Elvis's image was deliberate, and had begun even before he left for Germany. Elvis and the Colonel abandoned the notoriety of rock 'n' roll for the wider appeal of movies and pop music. In terms of financial success and overall popularity, they made the right decision. A single image sums up the change in Elvis: The ducktail that had been shorn when he went into the army never grew back.

CHAPTER EIGHT

ELVIS IS BACK

As for the fans, they've changed some but they're still there . . . .

The president of one fan club came to see me

and I hardly recognized her.

She's going to college now. I was surprised she looked me up.

She was more mature, but she

stopped by anyway.

ELVIS PRESLEY

EARLY 1960s

Elvis's discharge from the army resulted in a media blitz so manic that reporters began generating publicity about the publicity.

Anxious to resume his career, Elvis recorded and released an album in less than two months.

As soon as Sergeant Elvis Presley was discharged from the army, his recording company, RCA, and his manager, Colonel Tom Parker, wanted him to make a record. They let Elvis have only two weeks to readjust to civilian life, and then he had to go to Nashville for his first recording session in almost two years. Elvis was joined in the studio by his old friends guitarist Scotty Moore and drummer D.J. Fontana, but Bill Black, who had played doghouse bass for Elvis, was no longer part of his band. Moore, Black, and

Fans had been accustomed to gathering around Elvis's home ever since he had become a nationally known figure. After he returned from the army, they continued this ritual.

Fontana had been Elvis's backup musicians during most of his early career, but in the fall of 1957 Moore and Black resigned as regular members of Elvis's band. Money may have had a lot to do with it: Scotty and Bill were paid only $100 a week while they were in Memphis and $200 a week while they were on the road. The Colonel may have been responsible for the skimpy wages, but Elvis was never known to pay high salaries to the people who worked for him. Black eventually formed his own group, The Bill Black Combo, and in 1959 they recorded a popular song called "Smokie—Part 2." Moore continued to record with Elvis in the studio on a free-lance basis until 1969. D.J. Fontana, who had been recruited from *Louisiana Hayride*, had a separate arrangement with Elvis that allowed him more leeway in his career.

A welcome-home cake was sent to Elvis upon his release from the army. The cake was cleverly decorated with the titles of his number-one tunes.

Elvis clowns around on the drums between takes at a recording session. Photos such as these reveal Elvis's sense of humor, an element often missing from many accounts of his life.

Moore and Fontana were not the only musicians hired for the Nashville recording sessions: famed country pianist Floyd Cramer had signed on, and once again the Jordanaires sang backup vocals. During the first session Elvis cut a single featuring "Stuck on You" on one side and "Fame and Fortune" on the flip side. In early April Elvis returned to the RCA studio in Nashville to record the additional tracks necessary for an album. These two April recording sessions yielded some of the best work of his career. Elvis recorded his usual mix of rock, country, and R&B songs, including "Fever," which Peggy Lee had made famous two years earlier, and two rhythm-and-blues numbers, "Reconsider Baby" and "Such a Night." By the end of April, *Elvis Is Back* had been released. In less than two months, RCA had recorded and pressed a brand-new Elvis Presley album, and it was playing on the radio.

Not all of the songs Elvis recorded in Nashville were included on the album *Elvis Is Back*. Two of his most acclaimed ballads, "It's Now or Never" and "Are You Lonesome Tonight?" were held back for later release. Both became number-one singles. "Are You Lonesome Tonight?" was a clear departure from the kind of songs Elvis had been singing before he went into the army. In the 1920s Al Jolson had made this melancholy tune popular, but Elvis was probably more familiar with a 1959 version recorded by pop singer Jaye P. Morgan, who borrowed her arrangement from a 1950 rendition by the Blue Barron Orchestra. Colonel Parker is believed to have urged Elvis to record "Are You Lonesome Tonight?" even though it was unusual for him to interfere with Elvis's choice of music. The song perfectly suited Elvis's new image as a mainstream pop singer. Although it's a pop song, "Are You Lonesome Tonight?" did well on country music charts. Elvis didn't record another song that reached the country charts until 1968.

Elvis's poignant recording of "Are You Lonesome Tonight?" touched off a pop-music fad known as the answer record. At least eight singers recorded answers to Elvis's musical question. Singer Thelma Carpenter told Elvis, "Deep in your heart, you know who lied," and Jo Ann Perry swore that on her stage the curtain would never come down. She had strayed because of a "bad actor" who had "oh, such a good line."

Unfairly criticized by many before he entered the army, Elvis resurfaced after his tour of duty as a shining example of young adulthood. Even Congress noticed the difference. In March of 1960, Senator Estes Kefauver read a tribute to Elvis into the Congressional Record.

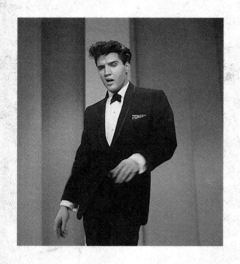

Elvis appeared on The Frank Sinatra Timex Show *for a record-breaking $125,000 fee.*

In a pairing of legends, Elvis sang Sinatra's "Witchcraft" while Sinatra crooned "Love Me Tender."

The television special presented Elvis as a patriotic and clean-cut young man.

"It's Now or Never" is based on the well-known Italian song "O Sole Mio." In 1949 Tony Martin recorded a pop version of "O Sole Mio." Elvis had heard Martin's rendition of the song, but he wanted new lyrics and a new arrangement of the tune before he was willing to record it. The new version was called "It's Now or Never," and it became one of Elvis's signature songs. During 1960 Elvis recorded another song that was based on an Italian tune. "Surrender" is a modern version of "Come Back to Sorrento," which had been recorded by Dean Martin (probably Elvis's favorite pop singer). Because "Surrender" is only one minute and 51 seconds long, it has the distinction of being one of the shortest songs ever to reach number one on the pop charts.

On May 12, 1960, Elvis appeared on television for the first time since his discharge from the army. He was a guest on *The Frank Sinatra Timex Show*. Colonel Parker had made the deal with the show's producers months before Elvis was released from active duty. He hoped that appearing with Sinatra would introduce Elvis as a pop singer to a wide audience made up of adults and pop enthusiasts as well as teenagers and country fans. Never one to take chances, the Colonel made sure Elvis would make a big splash by packing the studio audience with 400 members of one of Elvis's biggest fan clubs. The Colonel's plan succeeded: The program received phenomenal ratings, giving ABC a 41.5 share for that evening. This was a much larger television audience than Elvis had before he went into the army. He was paid $125,000 for a total of six minutes on the air.

Sammy Davis Jr., Peter Lawford, and Joey Bishop also appeared on the television special. In addition to these members of Sinatra's famed "Rat Pack," the cast included his daughter, Nancy, whom the gossip columns had recently linked romantically with Elvis. The show was subtitled "Welcome Home, Elvis," and in the opening segment Elvis wore his army uniform. Later he changed into a stylish but conservative black suit and joined Sinatra for a short duet. The former teen idol sang Sinatra's "Witchcraft" while Sinatra crooned Elvis's "Love Me Tender." In another segment Elvis sang both sides of his new single, "Stuck on You" and "Fame and Fortune." His conservative clothes, shorter hairstyle, and connection with the Rat Pack showed that Elvis's career was taking a new direction. When Elvis and Sinatra sang each other's songs, it was as though Sinatra was passing on his status as the pop idol of one generation to the idol of the next generation. The Voice, as Sinatra was known in the 1940s, was making way for the King.

Elvis's appearance on The Frank Sinatra Timex Show *was a symbolic beginning: His appearance, his style of music, and his desire to reach adult audiences signaled an image change. No longer a rebellious rock 'n' roller, Elvis had become a pop star.*

113

Vernon Presley helped Elvis manage his finances for most of his career.

Shortly after the Sinatra special, Elvis returned to Hollywood, where his personal appearance was toned down further to accommodate the image of a leading man.

Although his image had changed, Elvis returned to recording, television, and movies with the same degree of success he enjoyed before entering the army.

Shortly after his discharge from the army, Elvis added this Rolls-Royce Phantom V to his collection of exotic cars.

On March 25, 1961, Elvis performed live at the Bloch Arena in Pearl Harbor, Hawaii, at a benefit for the fund to build a memorial for the USS *Arizona*, which had been sunk in the harbor during World War II. Ticket prices for this performance ranged from three to ten dollars, with a hundred ringside seats reserved for people who donated $100. Elvis and Colonel Parker bought fifty special seats and donated them to patients at Tripler Hospital in Hawaii. Elvis's benefit raised more than $62,000 for the memorial fund. On March 30, the Hawaii House of Representatives passed Special Resolution 105 thanking Elvis and the Colonel.

Elvis performed at a benefit in Hawaii to raise money for the USS Arizona *Memorial in March of 1961. It was his last appearance before a live audience until 1969.*

There's no doubt that the benefit for the USS *Arizona* Memorial Fund made Elvis more acceptable to the adult audience that had shunned him when he was a rock 'n' roll rebel. But his career was not Elvis's only reason for wanting to help. He had a sensitive, generous nature, and throughout his entire life Elvis gave freely to charities and other worthy causes, whether he received publicity for it or not. Five years after this benefit concert, while he was in Hawaii filming *Paradise, Hawaiian Style*, Elvis visited the completed memorial and placed a wreath. Photographers and reporters rushed in to record the event, but Elvis sent them away. He did not want his visit to the memorial to become a publicity stunt.

After the 1961 concert in Hawaii, Elvis did not give another live performance until 1969, and he made no other television appearances after the Sinatra special until December 1968. Throughout most of the 1960s, if you wanted to see Elvis, you had to go to the movies.

CHAPTER NINE

A NEW IMAGE

He's the best-mannered star in Hollywood

and he's improved as a performer and has a determination

to be a fine actor.

He was smart enough to simmer down that

torrid act of his.

HEDDA HOPPER

EARLY 1960s

Not long after Elvis appeared on *The Frank Sinatra Timex Show*, he returned to Hollywood to begin shooting *G.I. Blues*. The movie is about a singer who is serving in the army in Germany. Producer Hal Wallis borrowed details from Elvis's own life to flesh out the script just as he did in the two earlier movies they made together. In *G.I. Blues* Elvis's character is stationed in the same place Elvis was, and he's a member of a tank division just as Elvis had been.

Elvis had plenty to smile about: At one point during this period, he was the highest-paid actor in Hollywood.

Art imitates life: In G.I. Blues, *Elvis played a singer who was serving in the army in Germany.*

G.I. Blues *revealed to movie audiences the new, clean-cut Elvis.*

G.I. Blues was the third and final movie Elvis made under his original contract with Hal Wallis. But as soon as he got to Hollywood, Colonel Parker began to negotiate another three-picture deal with Wallis. No one knows why Parker wanted to tie Elvis up with multipicture contracts instead of negotiating a contract for each movie based on the box-office performance of his most recent movie. Both he and Elvis probably would have made a lot more money that way. But in his second contract with Wallis (and in subsequent contracts), Elvis received a handsome salary and a percentage of the profits. At one point during the 1960s he was the highest-paid actor in Hollywood. Parker also did well for himself through his practice of complicating standard contracts with side deals and promotions. He also received a screen credit for each of Elvis's 31 movies. Most often he's sighted as a technical adviser.

Producer Hal Wallis devised the formula that Elvis's musical comedies would follow throughout the 1960s.

Elvis in Hollywood: One cynical director proclaimed, "There are only two surefire things in this business—Walt Disney and Elvis Presley."

G.I. Blues *helped soften Elvis's rebellious screen image by requiring him to play scenes with adorable infants.*

Like the movies Elvis made before he went into the army, *G.I. Blues* is based on events in his own life; but unlike those early movies, *G.I. Blues* is a musical comedy instead of a musical drama. The movie is aimed at a family audience, and Elvis's controversial performing style has been toned down. He still moves freely when he sings, but a troupe of long-legged dancers doing the latest dance craze behind him presents the only sensuous aspect of his performance. Elvis's character has also changed; he's older and looks more conservative. Even though most of the songs in *G.I. Blues* are fast-paced, they don't have the same hard-driving sound, sexual connotations, and emotional delivery as Elvis's earlier soundtrack recordings. Elvis's screen image had been deliberately softened. In one scene he sings a Bavarian-sounding folk tune during a children's puppet show, and in another he babysits an adorable infant.

Elvis's new, "softer" image became clear when he sang "Wooden Heart" to G.I. Blues *costar Juliet Prowse and a pair of puppets.*

Elvis's hair is short in *G.I. Blues* compared with his wild ducktail haircut, and it's also a different color than at the beginning of his career. Elvis's natural hair color was dark blond or light brown, although it usually looked darker because of the pomade he used to grease down his ducktail. But after the movie *Loving You* was released, Elvis had started to dye his hair jet black (which was the color of his mother's hair). The two movies that Elvis made after *Loving You* are in black and white, so the change wasn't obvious; but *G.I. Blues* and most of the other movies he made during the 1960s were in color, and the rich tones of Elvis's blue-black hair are very noticeable.

Elvis's natural hair color was dark blond (above), rather than the rich blue-black shade that he preferred (below).

Elvis with dancer Juliet Prowse. Elvis the Pelvis no longer swung his hips when he performed in his movies; a long-legged costar did it for him.

G.I. Blues *differed from Elvis's pre-army movies in that it was a musical comedy, not a musical drama.*

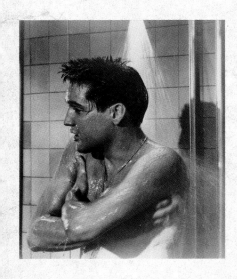

In *G.I. Blues* Robert Ivers and James Douglas play Elvis's pals, who are also members of his band. In many of Elvis's movies he has two or three buddies who are musicians. These movie sidekicks had their real-life counterparts in Elvis's buddy bodyguards, dubbed the "Memphis Mafia" by the press. They accompanied Elvis wherever he went.

Singer-dancer Juliet Prowse played Elvis's love interest in *G.I. Blues*. True to form, Elvis made her his love interest off-screen as well. At the time, Prowse had been romantically linked with Frank Sinatra, whom she had met on her previous movie, *Can-Can*. The press had a field day with stories claiming that Elvis had stolen Sinatra's girl. Although the relationship between Sinatra and Prowse doesn't seem to have amounted to much, Sinatra did visit her on the set during the production of *G.I. Blues*. Rumor has it that Elvis was in Prowse's dressing room one day when Sinatra came to see her. One of Elvis's buddy bodyguards knocked on the door to warn him that Sinatra was on the set, but Elvis thought it was a prank and ignored the warning. Even though he could laugh about it later, Elvis must have been pretty shocked when Sinatra actually walked into the dressing room. It wasn't the first or the last time Sinatra cropped up in Elvis's life. Sinatra had introduced Elvis on his television special after the singer was discharged from the army, and Elvis was romantically linked with Sinatra's daughter, Nancy, more than once during his career. Sinatra was originally offered a role in the western *Flaming Star* before the script was rewritten and Elvis got involved in the project. And in the 1970s both Elvis and Sinatra recorded "My Way," and each of them considered the song to be his personal anthem.

Elvis was linked romantically with Juliet Prowse during the production of G.I. Blues.

Despite Elvis's wholesome new image, *G.I. Blues* was banned in Mexico after his fans caused a riot at a theater in Mexico City, ripping out seats and breaking several windows. In addition to *G.I. Blues*, the Mexican government banned all future Elvis Presley movies. But in the United States, *G.I. Blues* was enormously successful; it ranked fourteenth in box-office receipts for 1960. The soundtrack album reached number one quickly and remained on the charts longer than any of Elvis's previous albums. Movie critics applauded the new Elvis; they were glad his sideburns were gone and thought he would find plenty of new fans among older women. Elvis didn't share the critics' enthusiasm for *G.I. Blues*. He felt there were too many musical numbers and that some of them made no sense within the context of the plot. He was also concerned that the quality of many of the songs was not as good as the music in his earlier movies.

Elvis relaxes between takes.

Elvis's next movie, the western *Flaming Star*, which was released in December 1960 by Twentieth Century Fox, gave him the chance to prove himself as a serious actor. The movie brought together some of Hollywood's most notable actors and creative personnel. In this tense drama Elvis was able to hold his own with veteran performers John McIntire and Dolores Del Rio, and his costar, a relative newcomer named Barbara Eden (who later starred in the television series *I Dream of Jeannie*). Director Don Siegel, who later won critical acclaim for his work on *Dirty Harry*, fashioned a strong statement on racial prejudice out of a script based on a popular novel by Clair Huffaker. Nunnally Johnson, a long-time Hollywood producer and screenwriter, cowrote the screenplay with Huffaker. Established composer Cyril Mockridge produced the background music.

Film veterans John McIntire and Dolores Del Rio played Elvis's parents.

Barbara Eden costarred with Elvis in the western drama Flaming Star.

Director Don Siegel, who went on to make Dirty Harry, *believed that having too many songs in* Flaming Star *would detract from the serious message.*

In an effort to prove himself a serious actor, Elvis sang only two songs in Flaming Star.

Elvis considered his role in Flaming Star *an important step in establishing himself as a legitimate actor. Unfortunately, the fans would not accept him in a movie not tailored to his image.*

In *Flaming Star* Elvis plays the half-breed son of a white settler and a Kiowa Indian. His character has the unlikely but romantic name Pacer Burton. A Kiowa uprising forces Pacer to choose sides between the white settlers and his mother's tribe. In addition to this dramatic conflict, the movie also shows the day-to-day prejudice Pacer experiences because of his half-caste status. This is a thinly veiled reference to the prejudice that blacks in the United States were experiencing during their struggle for civil rights.

A stuntman was hired to double for Elvis in the film, but Elvis was able to do most of his own action scenes.

Rumor had it that the role of Pacer Burton was originally written for Marlon Brando, adding to the idea that Elvis could have or should have followed in Brando's footsteps. As is often the case with stories about Elvis, the legend strays pretty far from what actually happened. In 1958 Twentieth Century Fox had purchased the rights to Clair Huffaker's novel before it was completed. The novel was then called *The Brothers of Flaming Arrow*, and it focused on two characters instead of one. Marlon Brando and Frank Sinatra were offered and accepted the roles of the two brothers. But later, negotiations with the two stars broke down. When the novel was completed, the title had been changed to *Flaming Lance*, and while the script was being written, the focus of the story shifted to one character. Elvis was the only actor offered the role of Pacer Burton as it was written in the screenplay. After going through several title changes— including *Flaming Heart*, *Black Star*, and *Black Heart*—the movie was released as *Flaming Star*.

Despite the participation of such industry greats as Dolores Del Rio, Nunnally Johnson, and Cyril Mockridge, *Flaming Star* was not a financial success. Audiences were disappointed because they had expected Elvis to perform several songs, but he sang only two. Some preview audiences saw a four-song version, but it was never released, probably because director Don Siegel thought that too many songs detracted from the movie's serious tone. Siegel may have been correct from an artistic point of view, since the movie got good reviews; but it was a box-office disappointment compared with *G.I. Blues*.

As Elvis's mother in Flaming Star, *actress Dolores Del Rio was returning to Hollywood films after an 18-year absence.*

Elvis, costar Hope Lange, director Philip Dunne, and other members of the crew celebrated a cast member's birthday during the production of Wild in the Country.

Elvis got only one more shot at serious acting, in *Wild in the Country*, which is one of his best movies. This modern-day drama set in the deep South was directed by Philip Dunne, who also participated in the production of such movie classics as *How Green Was My Valley* and *The Robe*. The screenplay was written by playwright Clifford Odets. Elvis stars as a young hothead named Glenn Tyler, who tries to straighten out

Playing Glenn Tyler was Elvis's last crack at serious acting for many years. As was the case with Flaming Star, Wild in the Country *did not live up to box-office expectations.*

his life after serving time in a juvenile hall. He becomes romantically involved with three women. Tuesday Weld, who was only 17 years old, plays an uneducated country girl who has an illegitimate child. She urges Tyler to stay with his own kind. Hope Lange costars as a psychologist who encourages Tyler to go to college to pursue a writing career. When Lange's character falls in love with her client, she causes a local scandal. Millie Perkins plays Tyler's childhood sweetheart. She puts his interests ahead of her own by encouraging him to get an education even if it means giving her up. The three women represent Glenn's past, present, and future. Of the three actresses, Tuesday Weld's sensuous performance best complements Elvis's smoldering on-screen presence.

Singer Pat Boone visited Elvis on the set during production.

Each of the three female characters in Wild in the Country *represented one aspect of Glenn Tyler's life. Here Tuesday Weld, as the sensual Norene, urges Glenn to stay close to his roots.*

Hope Lange costarred as psychologist Irene Sperry, who works hard to get Glenn into college. Irene's passion for the young man, however, jeopardizes her own career.

Millie Perkins portrayed Betty Lee Parsons, the childhood sweetheart who encourages Glenn to pursue his education even if it means she will lose him.

Christina Crawford made her acting debut in this movie as one of the girls in the town. This was long before she wrote her controversial best-seller, *Mommie Dearest*, and there's no record of her having made much of an impression on the movie's star. But Elvis and Tuesday grew close during the production of *Wild in the Country* and remained friends for several years. Elvis also dated the wardrobe girl, Nancy Sharp (they had met while *Flaming Star* was in production). In addition to his romantic interests, Elvis also became pals with Hope Lange. The press reported that Elvis suffered from a slight infection while the movie was being shot. Actually, his affliction was more embarrassing: Elvis had a severe case of boils on his backside. One day on location, Elvis was resting in his motel room, lying naked on his stomach with the afflicted area covered by hot washcloths and a sheet draped over his body. Hearing that Elvis was in pain, Hope Lange burst into his room to see if she could help. Elvis delicately explained what his problem was, but much to his chagrin, Hope lifted up his sheet. Greatly embarrassed by her actions, Elvis yelled out, "Whoa, there!" Even though he'd become a major Hollywood star, Elvis was still a shy country boy at heart.

No songs were included in the original script for this movie, but after the relatively poor showing *Flaming Star* made at the box office, six musical numbers were added to *Wild in the Country*. Only four of them made the final cut. In addition to the title tune that is sung over the opening credits, Elvis sings one song to each of the three women in the movie. Even with the musical numbers, *Wild in the Country* was a disappointment for Elvis's fans. Like *Flaming Star*, the movie didn't lose money at the box office; but it didn't make much either. Both Elvis and Tuesday Weld were voted the Damp Raincoat Award for the most disappointing performers of 1961 by the readers of *Teen* magazine. While this award would hardly ruin anyone's career, it showed Elvis and Colonel Tom exactly what kind of movie Elvis's most devoted fans wanted to see. After *Wild in the Country*, Elvis concentrated on making musical comedies.

The chemistry between Elvis and costar Tuesday Weld both on and off the set was unmistakable.

Elvis returned to musical comedy with *Blue Hawaii*, his most commercially successful film. Chad Gates, the son of a wealthy pineapple plantation owner, is nothing like the characters Elvis had played in the past (except that he had just gotten out of the army). Angela Lansbury costars as Elvis's mother, a Southern belle from a wealthy family with a lot of political clout. During this time in her career Lansbury specialized in portraying domineering matriarchs, even though she was only in her mid-thirties. The plot concerns Chad's reluctance to trade in his Hawaiian shirt for a business suit. Pressured by his parents to join his father in running the plantation, Chad chooses to play music on the beach with his native Hawaiian friends instead.

Blue Hawaii was directed by Norman Taurog, and Charles Lang Jr. was the cinematographer. The Hawaiian scenery is gorgeous; scenes were shot at Waikiki Beach, Hanauma Bay, and Ala Moana Park. The movie also features a huge cast of colorful characters. In response to his fans' cry for more songs, *Blue Hawaii* has 14 musical numbers, including one of Elvis's biggest hits, "Can't Help Falling in Love." Most of the songs fit well with the plot, and there's a wide range of musical styles—from the ultra-hip "Rock-a-Hula Baby" to the comical "Ito Eats."

Director Taurog was a competent Hollywood craftsman whose best-known effort was the 1938 hit *Boys Town*. He worked on nine of Elvis's movies—more than any other director. Many biographers claim that the mild-mannered Taurog was Elvis's favorite director because he was so sensitive to the needs of his star. During the filming of *Blue Hawaii*, Elvis let it be known that he was afraid of deep water. Many scenes in the movie were scheduled to be shot in or near the ocean, and director Taurog anticipated difficulties with Elvis. He gave the young actor the option of playing the scenes in the water, as called for in the script, or on the beach. Elvis appreciated Taurog's sensitivity toward his problem and worked to overcome it. Eventually he was able to get over his fear, and all the required scenes were shot with Elvis actually in the ocean.

Elvis poses for a surfing shot in Blue Hawaii. *Notice how the surfboard rests atop a plastic wave, exposing the "magic" of Hollywood moviemaking.*

While Elvis was trying to be cooperative, the Colonel seemed to be trying equally hard to be disagreeable. One rainy day, when Taurog had waited for many hours for a break in the weather, the Colonel alienated almost everyone on the set with an inexplicable power play. Just as the rain finally stopped and Taurog rolled the cameras on Elvis running out of the surf, Parker rushed in front of the camera, calling, "Cut, cut." This was a violation of proper etiquette on a movie set, where no one stops a scene except the director. Producer Hal Wallis and director Taurog were furious and demanded to know what could be important enough to cause Parker to halt the shot. Parker slyly pointed out that Elvis was wearing his own watch during the scene. The terms of his contract spelled out that Elvis was to provide no part of his wardrobe, including jewelry. If Wallis and Taurog wanted to use the take that had just been shot, they would have to pay Elvis $25,000 for providing his own wardrobe. Needless to say, Taurog had Elvis remove his watch and then reshot the scene.

Elvis kicks up some fun with a group of his costars from Blue Hawaii, *including Joan Blackman (left) and Jennie Maxwell (right).*

Elvis crooned fourteen songs in Blue Hawaii, *the highest grossing film of his career. In this publicity still, Elvis pretends to sing while Joan Blackman pretends to listen.*

Blue Hawaii was released during the Thanksgiving-Christmas holidays in 1961, and it grossed almost five million dollars. The soundtrack album was the fastest-selling album of that year. Unfortunately for Elvis, the success of *Blue Hawaii* restricted him to acting in musical comedies. The Colonel, Hal Wallis, and the other members of his management team used the tremendous box-office figures to convince a disappointed Elvis that this was the only kind of movie his fans wanted to see. After *Blue Hawaii*, Elvis made 23 more movies, all of which were financially successful. Even though Elvis had failed to become a serious actor, he was an extremely popular movie star.

Elvis checks his tan before splashing back into the water for one more take.

CHAPTER TEN

THE HIGHEST-PAID ACTOR IN MOVIES

People say Elvis's pictures aren't doing so good these days.

I tell you, we've made 22 pictures,

19 have been box-office successes, two haven't completed their runs yet,

and the other one hasn't been released.

How do you argue with this kind of success?

It's like telling Maxwell House to change their coffee formula

when the stuff is selling like no tomorrow.

COLONEL TOM PARKER

1966

Producer Hal Wallis, Colonel Parker, and Abe Lastfogel of the William Morris Agency were convinced that *Blue Hawaii* was a success because it had just the right mix of music, romance, and comedy. Parker supposedly told a scriptwriter that there were a quarter of a million die-hard Elvis fans who were willing to see each and every movie he made at least three times. Elvis and his management team had always catered to his fans: the Colonel offered special promotions to fan clubs and personally corresponded with the presidents of all the large fan clubs. After *Blue Hawaii*, Elvis concentrated on making the kind of movies his fans wanted to see.

Most of the movies Elvis made after 1961 were vehicles created to showcase his singing—musical comedies set in exotic locations such as Mexico or Hawaii, or in well-known vacation spots such as Las Vegas, Fort Lauderdale, or the Seattle World's Fair. When beach movies were popular, Elvis made *Blue Hawaii, Clambake,* and *Paradise, Hawaiian Style.* He made ski-resort movies when they were popular. He made a movie set in London and Antwerp when the discotheque scene was hot. In these movies Elvis plays a fun-loving ski instructor, boat captain, pilot, or race-car driver—who can also sing, of course. While Elvis may have been disappointed with these "Presley travelogues," as he called them, his fans felt that Elvis's charisma transcended the mediocre material he was given. When a long line formed outside the theater where one of Elvis's movies was playing, everyone knew the people had come to see Elvis and nothing else.

Elvis's musical vehicles put him to work in the most adventurous occupations: A boat captain in Girls, Girls, Girls ...

...a rodeo wrangler in Stay Away, Joe...

...an actor in Harum Scarum...

...a boxer in Kid Galahad...

...a race-car driver in Viva Las Vegas...

...a fashion photographer in Live a Little, Love a Little...

...a carnival worker in Roustabout...

...and an airplane pilot in It Happened at the World's Fair. *But no matter what the job, Elvis's character just happened to be able to sing!*

Speaking of singing...Elvis often sang to his beautiful costars in the most offbeat, out-of-the-way locations: To Ann-Margret on a diving board in Viva Las Vegas...

...to Jocelyn Lane in the shower in Tickle Me...

...to (top) Julie Parrish, Suzanna Leigh, Marianna Hill, (bottom) Irene Tsu, and Linda Wong in a grass hut in Paradise, Hawaiian Style...

...to Nancy Sinatra inside a crystal ball in Speedway...

...and to Donna Douglas on an old-fashioned riverboat in Frankie and Johnny.

138

In the movies Elvis made before he went into the army, he usually sang onstage because his character was an up-and-coming singer. After *Blue Hawaii*, the musical numbers are integrated into the story, and Elvis's character bursts into song at a moment's notice, wherever he happens to be. He sings in cars, on boats, in airplanes, on the beach, and even on an amusement park ride. Although Hollywood musicals had presented songs in this way for many years, Elvis thought it was too unrealistic. He was uncomfortable with his character breaking into song at any time and in any place.

Elvis's movies were vehicles tailored to suit his specific musical talents, much like Bob Hope and Bing Crosby's The Road to Bali *had been built around their talents.*

Elvis's vehicles fit comfortably in the same movie genre as those colorful but campy beach comedies such as How to Stuff a Wild Bikini.

In Hollywood a movie that is built around a particular star is known as a vehicle. Many well-respected musical and comedy stars have appeared in vehicles, including Fred Astaire, Ginger Rogers, Bob Hope, and Bing Crosby. In the 1960s pop stars often appeared in vehicles. Frankie Avalon and Herman's Hermits starred in movies created to showcase their talents. Dick Dale and the Del-Tones, the Hondells, the Pyramids, and the Kingsmen all made vehicles with a surfin' sound. Other rock groups appeared in movies that featured their sound, including the Turtles, Freddie and The Dreamers, Gary Lewis and The Playboys, the Supremes, the Righteous Brothers, and the Four Seasons. Even the Beatles made movies like *A Hard Day's Night* and *Help!* to showcase soundtrack albums.

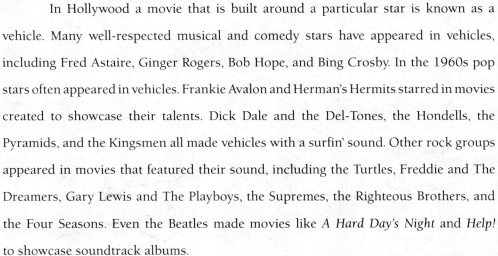

When the beach comedies starring pop singer Frankie Avalon and former Mousketeer Annette Funicello became popular, Elvis also hit the beach in his movies for some fun in the sun.

Most rock 'n' roll movies were meant strictly for a teen audience, but Elvis's musical comedies are family fare. The casts include children as well as older characters. Although most of Elvis's vehicles were standard 1960s teen movies, a memorable few had superior casts, good direction, high-quality songs, scripts that made sense, and first-rate production values.

The Beatles' films, including Help!, *are the most artistic and intelligent examples of those 1960s rock 'n' roll musicals aimed at younger audiences.*

Elvis graciously signed autographs for his fans in Florida during the filming of Follow That Dream.

Follow That Dream is based on the novel *Pioneer, Go Home* by Richard Powell. The movie is more of a satire than a romantic comedy, although plenty of sparks fly between Elvis and his costars, Anne Helm and Joanna Moore. In this movie Elvis isn't an irresistible romantic hero; he's a country boy whose family decides to homestead on an unopened stretch of highway in Florida. Claiming squatter's rights, they open a small business renting out fishing equipment. A welfare organization investigates the family and threatens to take away the younger children on the grounds that they are living in a bad moral climate. Elvis helps plead their case in court, and the family is kept together. In this movie Elvis plays a character who is not even remotely like himself: a bumbling fellow who isn't too quick on the uptake. The critics noticed his natural flair for comic timing.

Follow That Dream was shot almost totally in Florida, making use of a bank in Ocala and the courthouse in Inverness. Part of the plot focuses on a couple of bad guys who take advantage of the family and set up a gambling operation on their property. Dice tables and other gambling equipment were needed for the set, but gambling was illegal in Florida, and no one knew where the necessary props could be obtained quickly and legally. But one day a member of the Chamber of Commerce of Florida and a couple of real-life mobsters, who chose to remain anonymous, showed up on location with the needed items. In *Follow That Dream*, Elvis sings only five songs rather than the ten or more tunes he usually performs in his musicals. Even though the title tune is excellent, his fans wanted more songs, and the movie didn't do as well at the box office as most of Elvis's other movies.

An excellent supporting cast, including twins Robin and Gavin Koon, Anne Helm, and two-time Oscar nominee Arthur O'Connell, made Follow That Dream *one of Elvis's best comedies.*

Follow That Dream *pokes fun at everything from welfare organizations to psychiatry.*

In 1963 the world's fair was held in Seattle, Washington. To celebrate the fair and take advantage of a well-publicized event, MGM decided to make *It Happened at the World's Fair*. Elvis stars with Gary Lockwood in this musical comedy about a pair of pilots whose small plane has been attached for nonpayment of bills. The two men end up in Seattle looking for jobs. At the world's fair Elvis finds a little girl who has been separated from her family. While Elvis searches the fairgrounds for the little girl's father, the movie audience gets to see the Monorail, the Space Needle, the Skyride, the Dream Car Exhibit, and many other attractions of the fair. Vicky Tiu, who made her movie debut in *It Happened at the World's Fair*, plays the lost child. Kurt Russell plays another child in this movie, but his character doesn't think much of Elvis and kicks him hard in the shins. Ironically, when Russell grew up, he starred as Elvis in the 1979 television biography produced by Dick Clark.

Elvis and costar Gary Lockwood hitch a ride to Seattle, hoping to find luck and work at the World's Fair.

While *It Happened at the World's Fair* was in production, the entertainment press announced that Elvis was to have the starring role of country singer Hank Williams in his movie biography, *Your Cheatin' Heart*. But nothing ever came of it. No one knows whether the Colonel and the people at William Morris were reluctant to risk a possible flop with Elvis in a different kind of role or the deal just fell through. This would not be the last time Elvis turned down a juicy part, but it was a loss for music fans, who would have enjoyed seeing Elvis in the life story of another musical legend. The movie was eventually made with George Hamilton in the role of country music's most beloved performer.

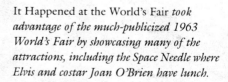

It Happened at the World's Fair: *Elvis sings the lullaby "Cotton Candy Land" to Vicky Tiu.*

It Happened at the World's Fair *took advantage of the much-publicized 1963 World's Fair by showcasing many of the attractions, including the Space Needle where Elvis and costar Joan O'Brien have lunch.*

Elvis's wardrobe for It Happened at the World's Fair, *which included this authentic flight jacket and pilot's cap, cost almost $10,000.*

For an authentic Latin sound, the Four Amigos accompanied Elvis on a number of songs in Fun in Acapulco.

Elvis and costar Ursula Andress made the most of Fun in Acapulco, *though critics were less than kind in their reviews.*

Once again, Elvis was paired with a cute child in an effort to appeal to a family audience. Here, Larry Domasin looks adoringly at Elvis and Ursula Andress.

In *Fun in Acapulco* Elvis plays a trapeze artist who's afraid of heights because his partner was severely injured in an accident. He takes a job as a lifeguard in an Acapulco hotel, where he meets the resort's social director, played by Ursula Andress. The exteriors for this romantic adventure were shot on location, but Elvis never traveled to Mexico; all of his scenes were shot on the Paramount lot in Hollywood. Just before production on the movie began, a newspaper story misquoted Elvis as saying he disliked Mexico and the Mexican people. Because of this and the fact that many of Elvis's movies had been banned in Mexico, producer Hal Wallis felt it was unsafe for Elvis to shoot his scenes on location.

Early in his Hollywood career, Elvis had developed a reputation for dating his costar while a movie was in production. Rumors about Elvis's crushes on actresses were circulated constantly in fan magazines and elsewhere in the press. Much of what was said was obviously manufactured for its publicity value, but some of the rumors were undoubtedly true or almost true. To his credit, Colonel Parker kept information about Elvis's personal life to a minimum. He leaked just enough details about Elvis's Hollywood life to keep the media away from Priscilla, who was actually living at Graceland, although she and Elvis were not yet married.

Although critics claim Elvis's films featured few dynamic costars, Ursula Andress made a formidable love interest in Fun in Acapulco.

Because of his reputation, Elvis had to be careful around his leading lady, Ursula Andress, during the making of *Fun in Acapulco*. She had been James Bond's girl in the spy thriller *Dr. No.*, but this was her first American movie. Andress was married to director-actor John Derek (who later married actress Bo Derek). Rumor has it that Derek was incredibly jealous of any man who came near his wife, and so he visited the set frequently to keep an eye on her. While *Fun in Acapulco* was in production, Derek gave Andress a customized car with "Baby, You're Indispensable" emblazoned on the steering wheel.

Fun in Acapulco became a top grosser for 1963, the year it was released. But movie reviewers thought it was pretty lightweight. What did they expect from a movie that includes a song called "No Room to Rhumba in a Sports Car"? *Variety* said that Elvis was "deserving of better material," while other reviewers recognized that he was simply catering to his most devoted fans. The Beatles were among the throngs of Elvis's fans who enjoyed *Fun in Acapulco*; they took time out from their first American tour to see the movie in Miami.

While some of Elvis's movies are better than others, *Kissin' Cousins*, which was released in 1964, is generally considered to be Elvis's worst movie. This musical comedy was produced by Sam Katzman, who had a reputation for churning out low-budget movies on short schedules. Estimates on how long it took to shoot the movie vary, but everyone agrees that it took less than three weeks. The movie was budgeted at $800,000, compared with the 4-million-dollar budget of *Blue Hawaii*. Little time was allotted for rehearsal, even for the musical numbers.

Kissin' Cousins, costarring Yvonne Craig, *has the distinction of being one of Elvis's worst movies. Produced by King of the Quickies, Sam Katzman, the film's low budget is embarrassingly apparent.*

The outrageous story line features Elvis in a dual role. He plays an Air Force officer who tries to persuade a Tennessee mountain family to allow a missile base to be built on their land, and he also plays a son in the family. As Officer Josh Morgan, Elvis appears on screen with black hair; as Jodie Tatum, he wears a dark blond wig, which was closer to his natural hair color. The dark-haired Elvis wins the affections of Yvonne Craig, while the blond Elvis courts Cynthia Pepper. The other characters in the movie parody Southerners: There are barefoot hillbillies, moonshiners, lazy hound dogs, man-chasing mountain girls, and pipe-smoking mammies. No wonder the movie has been criticized so often. Maureen Reagan, the former president's daughter, has the dubious distinction of appearing as the most embarrassing character in *Kissin' Cousins*; she plays Lorraine, the leader of the Kittyhawks, a group of hillbilly women who are desperate for husbands.

146

While singing "One Boy, Two Little Girls" in Kissin' Cousins, *Elvis romances a pair of down-home,
country girls, played by Yvonne Craig and Pam Austin.*

147

Elvis had a dual role in Kissin' Cousins: *As Josh Morgan (left) he courted Yvonne Craig; as Jodie Tatum (right), he won the affections of Cynthia Pepper.*

In addition to an offensive cast of characters, the songs for *Kissin' Cousins* sound as though they came off an assembly line. Katzman decided that since the movie had a country theme, the songs should be recorded in Nashville rather than in Hollywood, where Elvis's other soundtrack albums had been made. But the movie's mediocre tunes are some songwriter's misguided interpretations of country music. The nine songs in the movie, including "Barefoot Ballad," "Pappy, Won't You Please Come Home," and "Kissin' Cousins," sound nothing like the country music that was being produced in Nashville at the time.

Thanks to the magic of Hollywood, Elvis faces off with himself in Kissin' Cousins.

The exteriors for the movie were shot at Big Bear Lake in California. Right after the location shooting was finished, Elvis was involved in what could have been a fatal accident. While driving down the mountain from Big Bear Lake in a recreational vehicle, Elvis was stunned when the brakes gave out completely. A car carrying some of the movie crew was traveling ahead of Elvis's RV, and the driver was forced to speed up to keep ahead of the huge vehicle lumbering down the mountain behind it. The road was too narrow for Elvis to pass the car, and a sheer drop on one side made the speed at which both vehicles were traveling very dangerous. Elvis used the gears to maneuver the RV down the mountain road, while the car managed to stay just ahead of him. When Elvis reached the bottom of the hill, he had to keep going until the vehicle eventually slowed to a stop. If Elvis had not been such a competent driver, *Kissin' Cousins* might have been his last legacy to his fans.

Kissin' Cousins was the first of Elvis's low-budget movies. After he made this movie, the shooting schedules for his musical comedies seemed to grow shorter and the budgets smaller. Some people say that Colonel Parker felt that Elvis's popularity as a movie star was waning, so he began to seek out producers who could lower production costs. He also looked for resorts and hotels that would allow the cast and crew to stay for free. There's no proof that the Colonel actually intended to lower the quality of Elvis's movies; the decline in production values that went along with smaller budgets and shorter schedules probably resulted from decreased box-office receipts.

The explosive Ann-Margret was Elvis's most dynamic costar.

Elvis was not restricted to working for Hal Wallis because the contracts they signed were not exclusive. Elvis also worked for MGM, United Artists, and Allied Artists. *Viva Las Vegas* was produced by MGM and released in 1964. Even though this musical comedy is basically another "Presley travelogue," Elvis's dynamic costar, Ann-Margret, made it a cut above the others. The exteriors were shot in and around Las Vegas at locations such as the Flamingo and Tropicana hotels, and the drag strip at Henderson, Nevada.

Ann-Margret was known at the time as "the female Elvis Presley" because of her sensual dancing style. The musical numbers in *Viva Las Vegas* are sparked by an electricity not found in other Elvis movies. The high-voltage rhythm-and-blues number "What'd I Say" recalls a younger, more dangerous Elvis. Many people feel that the on-screen chemistry between Elvis and Ann-Margret was a reflection of their off-screen romance.

Of all his relationships with costars, Elvis's romance with Ann-Margret was probably the most serious. During the production of *Viva Las Vegas*, the publicity mill ground out story after story every time Elvis and his costar showed up together at a Las Vegas restaurant or club. They shared a passion for motorcycles and occasionally rode together, but they had to be especially careful because an accident involving either one of them would have delayed production on the movie.

Known as "the female Elvis Presley" for her sensual dancing style, Ann-Margret perfectly complemented Elvis's high-powered musical performances.

Elvis and Ann-Margret pose for publicity shots to promote the "What'd I Say" musical number from Viva Las Vegas. *Said one reviewer, "There's nothing wrong with the motor in our boy. It's revved up as usual."*

Elvis romanced Ann-Margret both on and off the screen, adding to his reputation for dating his leading ladies. The two remained friends long after their romantic relationship was over.

Ann-Margret and Elvis duet with "The Lady Loves Me."

The publicity surrounding the romance was a dream come true for the producers of *Viva Las Vegas*, but it must have been difficult for Priscilla, who was kept hidden from the public at Graceland. Even Elvis's hometown newspaper, the *Memphis Press-Scimitar*, ran stories with such sensational headlines as "It Looks Like Romance for Elvis and Ann-Margret" and "Elvis Wins Love of Ann-Margret."

Viva Las Vegas was banned on the tiny Mediterranean island of Gozo for being too explicit...

When *Viva Las Vegas* was first in production, Elvis was not happy to be teamed with Ann-Margret. Someone on the production team had dated her on another movie location and was still smitten by her charm and beauty. When he assisted with photography, he seemed to favor Ann-Margret over Elvis, giving her more close-ups and better camera angles. When Elvis complained to the Colonel, he came to the rescue, and the crew member was soon chastised. When Elvis realized that Ann-Margret was unaware of the preferential treatment she was getting, he immediately turned on the charm and the two became fast friends. Although their romance didn't develop into a long-term relationship, Elvis and Ann-Margret remained friends for the rest of his life. Elvis married Priscilla, and Ann-Margret married actor Roger Smith, but Elvis still sent Ann-Margret flowers in the shape of a guitar on the opening night of every one of her Las Vegas engagements.

The film was originally titled Only Girl in Town. *In England and Europe, it was released as* Love in Las Vegas.

...but set box-office records in many other parts of the world.

In *Viva Las Vegas* Elvis plays a race-car driver who takes a job as a waiter at the Flamingo Hotel to earn money to enter the Las Vegas Grand Prix. Ann-Margret is a swimming instructor who's romanced by both Elvis's character and another dashing race-car driver played by Cesare Danova. (Teri Garr also appears briefly as a showgirl.) The movie was directed by George Sidney, a veteran of many Hollywood musicals, who integrates the musical numbers into the story line so that they never seem out of place or merely tacked on.

The Mexican government allowed *Viva Las Vegas* to be released there. The only place it was banned was on Gozo, a small Mediterranean island. (A Roman Catholic priest from the island thought the movie was indecent and asked his congregation to boycott it.) *Viva Las Vegas* was a blockbuster everywhere else. It set box-office records in Tokyo, Manila, and other parts of the Far East, helping to make Elvis the world's biggest star.

Ann-Margret and Elvis liked to ride motorcycles—a pasttime that panicked the producers for fear that one or both of the film's valuable stars would be involved in an accident.

153

Joan Freeman played Elvis's love interest in Roustabout, *but her screen presence was no match for costar Barbara Stanwyck's.*

Elvis tries his luck at seducing Joan Freeman against the colorful backdrop of the carnival midway. Joan just looks skeptical.

Elvis sang his customary ten songs in the film, of which "Little Egypt" became the best known.

Elvis's sixteenth movie, *Roustabout*, featured a cast of big-name stars, including Barbara Stanwyck, Leif Erickson, and Jack Albertson. Raquel Welch made her movie debut in this film; she plays a college girl. Richard Kiel, who later played Jaws in the James Bond adventures *Moonraker* and *The Spy Who Loved Me*, is the carnival strong man. This musical romance with a touch of melodrama was produced by Hal Wallis for Paramount and released in 1964. Wallis's solid reputation in Hollywood often helped him line up major stars for Elvis's movies. Legend has it that Wallis first approached Mae West for Stanwyck's role, but she declined the offer. The combination of Elvis Presley and Mae West would have been sensational, although West's larger-than-life screen presence might have detracted from the story line. Stanwyck's image as a tough, independent woman was better suited to the character. Edith Head, Hollywood's most illustrious costume designer, did the wardrobe for the movie. She even designed a special pair of form-fitting jeans for Stanwyck.

Roustabout is set against the colorful backdrop of a small American carnival, with Elvis starring as a rakish carny hand who has a knack for finding trouble. Barbara Stanwyck discovers his singing talent and uses him to attract crowds to the midway. When filming first started there was tension between the two stars, but eventually they came to like and respect each other. Elvis said that working with Stanwyck encouraged him to become a better actor.

Ten songs were written for the movie, but "Little Egypt" is by far the best known. Elvis sings this tune while a hootchy-kootchy dancer shimmies on stage. The original Little Egypt was a real-life belly dancer who created a sensation at the Chicago World's Fair in 1893. After the movie was released, another professional dancer who called herself Little Egypt sued Paramount, RCA, and Elvis Presley Music for damages to her reputation. She sought a restraining order to prevent the distribution of the movie and the sale of the soundtrack album. She lost her case, but the publicity it generated helped promote both the movie and the album.

Since Elvis's musical comedies were relatively inexpensive to produce but always profitable, Hal Wallis sometimes put them up as collateral for financing other movies. He used the potential profits of *Roustabout* as a guarantee for the backers who invested in his production of *Becket*, which won an Academy Award for best adapted screenplay. It's said that after Elvis stopped making movies, he complained bitterly that his producer had just been using him.

Oscar-winning fashion designer Edith Head created a pair of special jeans for Barbara Stanwyck for this film. Head exclaimed, "These blue denims are undoubtedly the most expensive and glamorous blue jeans ever designed."

Barbara Stanwyck headed a top-notch cast in Roustabout, *although her role was first offered to another legend, Mae West.*

*Ad copy for this musical described Elvis's character, Charlie Rogers, as "a roving, restless, reckless roustabout."
Although Charlie was tougher than most, he was no match for those sexy, alienated youths of
Elvis's pre-army films.*

Elvis winds up in a Ft. Lauderdale jail with a bevy of beauties in Girl Happy.

In the early 1960s Ft. Lauderdale, Florida, became the vacation spot for college students during spring break, with thousands of students descending on the coastal city every year. Always ready to cash in on a fad, Hollywood produced several movie musicals about college kids vacationing in Florida. One of these movies, *Girl Happy*, stars Elvis. Shelley Fabares, who played the eldest daughter on the television series *The Donna Reed Show*, costars with Elvis as the college-age daughter of a Chicago nightclub owner. When she decides to vacation in Florida, her father hires Elvis, who plays a singer, and his band to spy on his daughter while she has fun in the sun. Fabares was no stranger to the pop music scene; she had recorded a number-one hit in 1962 called "Johnny Angel." Her role opposite Elvis in *Girl Happy* was a success, and she costarred with him in two other movies, *Spinout* and *Clambake*. Elvis said later that she was his favorite costar, but the two stars were not involved romantically. Fabares dated producer Lou Adler during the production of *Girl Happy* and later married him.

In *Girl Happy*, the members of Elvis's band are played by Joby Baker, Gary Crosby (Bing's son), and Jimmy Hawkins. These buddies share in crazy antics with Elvis. Only Crosby had any musical talent, but that did not detract from the charm of this trio of wacky characters.

Elvis's close buddies and members of his band are played by (left to right) Gary Crosby, Jimmy Hawkins, and Joby Baker.

156

In addition to accompanying Elvis onstage, Hawkins, Crosby, and Baker join Elvis in a variety of girl-chasing antics.

Playing the wolf while singing "Wolf Call," Elvis lures Shelley Fabares into his lair.

Shelley Fabares, who would later appear in Spinout *and* Clambake, *costarred as Elvis's love interest in* Girl Happy.

The actors who played Elvis's backup musicians rarely had any musical ability, but that didn't matter. What was important was that everyone looked like they were having fun.

Most of the songs in *Girl Happy* are solid Elvis tunes, especially the low-down blues number "Wolf Call" and the easy-sounding ballad "Puppet on a String." But one song in this movie probably ranks as the worst tune Elvis ever recorded. "Do the Clam" was written to accompany a dance called the Clam that was created especially for the movie by choreographer David Winter. He was the dance director for the rock 'n' roll television program *Hullabaloo* and probably should have known better than to try to invent a dance. During the mid-1960s several dance crazes swept the nation, including the Monkey, the Pony, and the Swim; but the Clam didn't catch on.

Elvis averaged three movies a year between 1960 and 1969, and a soundtrack album was released in conjunction with each movie. After 1964 the Colonel insisted that Elvis record only soundtrack albums. Unfortunately, the music for these movies was often not as good as it should have been, and the production quality of the albums wasn't consistent. Some of them sound almost like amateur productions. The soundtrack albums were usually recorded in two or three all-night sessions. Apparently, neither Colonel Parker nor anyone at RCA or Hill and Range was interested in sinking money into good material for Elvis when mediocre albums were easy to produce and sold well. Since the system worked to everyone's advantage, there was no reason to change it.

The albums and the movies promoted each other. The release of a soundtrack album reminded fans that a movie would soon be appearing in their neighborhood theaters, while the movie served as a full-color, full-length advertisement for the soundtrack album. Unfortunately, the executives at RCA and Colonel Parker released Elvis's albums too rapidly. One of Elvis's soundtrack albums was likely to come out while an earlier one was still on the charts. The standard practice is to get as much mileage as possible from one album before releasing the next.

Not surprisingly, Elvis's control of the pop, country, and rhythm-and-blues charts faded during the 1960s. After 1960 Elvis didn't have a song on the country charts until 1968; and after 1963 he would never again place a record on the R&B charts. Elvis was able to coast on his reputation until about 1965. That year, he had only one top-10 single, "Crying in the Chapel," which he actually recorded in 1960. His soundtrack albums placed in the top 10, but just barely. In 1966 only one of Elvis's singles, "Love Letters," made it to the top 20. He had no top-20 recordings in 1967.

Grab your barefoot baby .... C'mon everybody, do the Clam.

CHAPTER ELEVEN

THE END
OF ONE CAREER

I'm tired of playing a guy who would be in a fight

and would start singing to the guy

he was beating up.

ELVIS PRESLEY

1969

By the end of the 1960s, audiences and critics pretty much knew what to expect from an Elvis Presley movie. There would be a group of happy-go-lucky characters cavorting in a well-known resort or vacation spot with little on their minds except music and romance. In 1967 a review of *Easy Come, Easy Go* in *Variety* pointed out the formula, but admitted that the movies were often well made and lots of fun to watch.

Elvis practically phoned in his part for the lackluster Clambake.

Live a Little, Love a Little *suffered from a far-fetched story line.*

Producer Hal Wallis ended his association with Elvis and Colonel Tom Parker in 1966 after the production of *Easy Come, Easy Go*, but Elvis continued to make movies for other studios. Some of these movies are not up to par, especially the lackluster *Double Trouble* and *Clambake*, and the ridiculously far-fetched *Live a Little, Love a Little*. In 1968 Elvis decided to stop making movies as soon as he had fulfilled his existing contracts. Curiously, his last three movies, all released in 1969, broke away from the pattern of his other films. Why Elvis made this change so late in his acting career is anyone's guess. Perhaps he still had the desire to mature as an actor and had decided to make another attempt at serious roles before he left Hollywood. Or maybe the Colonel thought a different kind of story line might score big at the box office. Most likely, the deals were simply too good for the Colonel to pass up. Whatever the reason, *Charro!*, *The Trouble with Girls*, and *Change of Habit* are different from Elvis's other movies.

Rudy Vallee, the singing idol of one generation, croons a tune through his trademark megaphone, while Elvis, the idol of another generation, accompanies him on the guitar. The two singing legends teamed up for Live a Little, Love a Little.

Double Trouble *attempted to cash in on the discotheque scene, which was considered hip at the time. Too bad that the script missed the mark by a mile.*

Elvis took the title role in the gritty western Charro!

Charro! is a low-budget western with Elvis in the title role as a former outlaw. The supporting cast was made up of many unknown actors, some of whom went on to become television stars, including Victor French (*Little House on the Prairie*), James Sikking (*Hill Street Blues*), James Almanzar (*The High Chaparral*), Paul Brinegar (*Rawhide*), and Harry Landers (*Ben Casey*). The story follows Charro, who's now on the side of law and order, as he stands up to the members of his old gang when they try to frame him for the theft of a valuable cannon that belongs to the Mexican government. Elvis's role is not glamorous. Throughout the movie he looks unkempt and wears the same dusty outfit. Elvis is barely recognizable behind a scruffy beard, and he sings no songs other than the title tune, which is heard during the opening credits. The poster used to advertise the movie exploits this new turn in Elvis's movie career, claiming that *Charro!* is "a different kind of role . . . a different kind of man."

The background music for *Charro!* was scored and conducted by Hugo Montenegro, who received critical acclaim for his memorable theme for Clint Eastwood's Italian western, *The Good, the Bad, and the Ugly*. The director of *Charro!*, Charles Marquis Warren, who also produced and scripted the movie, was obviously trying to capture the tense atmosphere and gritty look of the Italian westerns that were so popular in the 1960s. Elvis's character copied Clint Eastwood's beard and rugged appearance, and Hugo Montenegro's score made the movie sound like a spaghetti western; but Warren, who had directed and produced television westerns, lacked the vision to make *Charro!* as good as a Clint Eastwood movie. It's slow moving and dull, and Elvis's fans didn't like the movie very much.

Noted European actress Ina Balin (right) costarred as Elvis's love interest—a welcome change from the unknown ingenues who had danced their way through some of his musical comedies.

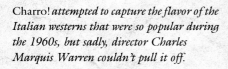

Charro! attempted to capture the flavor of the Italian westerns that were so popular during the 1960s, but sadly, director Charles Marquis Warren couldn't pull it off.

"Charro! *A different kind of role...a different kind of man.*"

Little Anissa Jones, later Buffy on television's Family Affair, *made her film debut in* The Trouble with Girls. *She charmed everyone on the set by knitting little sweaters for her pet gopher snakes.*

The Trouble with Girls is charming in an offbeat way. The story takes place in the 1920s and is about a chautauqua, which was a traveling school that featured classes in culture, reading, music, and other subjects. Chautauquas traveled from town to town, bringing culture to rural areas and isolated villages. The name derives from Chautauqua, New York, where a 12-day study program for Sunday school teachers had been set up in 1873.

Sheree North, who has a secondary role in The Trouble with Girls, *is involved in a murder.*

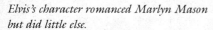

Elvis's character romanced Marlyn Mason but did little else.

As the manager of the chautauqua, Elvis is at the center of the movie. But the story line is largely taken up by the secondary characters: A couple of poor kids desperately want to be in the talent competition sponsored by the chautauqua; there is an illicit love affair that ends in murder; and there are other misadventures that have little to do with Elvis's character. In one of these subplots, Dabney Coleman (who had already established his humorously unsavory character in his first movie) appears as a drugstore owner who chases women, but masks his activities with his slippery manner.

Elvis's role is to develop a romance with the character played by Marlyn Mason. Elvis doesn't appear at all in the first third of *The Trouble with Girls*; then he strolls in wearing a gleaming white suit and dapper white hat. More handsome than ever, his hair is longer, and he has sideburns that are more in keeping with the fashion of the 1960s than the 1920s. Despite Elvis's great looks, his character is little more than a plot device that ties the various subplots together.

The seldom-used subtitle of The Trouble with Girls *is* And How to Get Into It.

Elvis starred as the manager of a Chautauqua, "the rolling college of musical knowledge."

A number of well-known character actors, including Edward Andrews, supported Elvis in this offbeat musical.

Elvis's hairstyle and sideburns looked up-to-date in The Trouble with Girls, *which the ad campaigns exploited with catchlines like, "This is Elvis '69—His New Look."*

Elvis's last feature film is a melodrama called *Change of Habit*. His costar is television favorite Mary Tyler Moore. Elvis plays a devoted doctor who works in a clinic in a big-city slum. Three young nuns, including Moore, are assigned to the ghetto to do social work. They decide to exchange their old-fashioned habits for modern dress, and Elvis falls in love with Moore, not realizing that she's a nun. In the final scene she must choose between Elvis and the Church; but the movie is a cliffhanger, and the audience is left not knowing which path she chooses.

Jane Elliott, Mary Tyler Moore, and Barbara McNair costarred as a trio of nuns who exchange their habits for more casual dress.

Between her TV stints with Dick Van Dyke and Ed Asner, Mary Tyler Moore costarred with the King in Change of Habit.

Mary Tyler Moore has always spoken kindly of Elvis, stating he was one of the nicest men she has ever worked with...a true gentleman.

Casting aside the adventurous occupations usually assigned to his characters, Elvis starred as a ghetto doctor in this melodrama.

Although he was used to playing free-spirited characters, Elvis seems right at home in the part of a well-respected professional man. He sings only a few songs in *Change of Habit*, including the popular hit "Rubberneckin'." For the most part, the songs fit in naturally with the story line, and movie critics commented on Elvis's relaxed, fluid performance. *Change of Habit* showed a profit at the box office, but it made an even bigger splash on television when it was shown on NBC's *Friday Night at the Movies* in 1972.

Elvis was anxious to fulfill his movie contracts and refocus his energy on music. His last role as an actor was in Change of Habit.

Mary Tyler Moore returned to television after Change of Habit, *and Elvis returned to live performances.*

In 1974, Barbra Streisand supposedly offered Elvis the male lead in her remake of A Star Is Born. Some sources claim that the Colonel ruined the deal by demanding an outrageous salary for Elvis. Whatever happened, Elvis missed his chance at a serious role—an opportunity he had coveted for most of his Hollywood career. The role went to singer Kris Kristofferson.

Despite the decline in Elvis's box-office receipts at the end of the 1960s, none of his movies ever lost money. Everyone involved in Elvis's Hollywood career benefited financially. Elvis's movies were planned so that 50 percent of the total budget was allotted for his salary, and he also received a percentage of the profits. Parker got 25 percent of Elvis's gross income and whatever he could negotiate as technical adviser. Abe Lastfogel of William Morris received 10 percent off the top of all of Elvis's movie deals.

Despite the opinions of his critics, Elvis's star on Hollywood Boulevard was well deserved.

The critics may not have found much to praise in Elvis's movies, but they certainly are no worse than other 1960s teen movies, and many of them are much better because of the good solid tunes on the soundtrack. After the revolutionary sound and raw energy of Elvis's rock 'n' roll music during the 1950s, it was difficult for many people to accept the mellow pop sound of Elvis's music after his discharge from the army. His 1950s image as a young rebel who defied conventions was a hard act to follow, even for Elvis. The singing movie star seemed like a weak substitute for Elvis's rebellious rock 'n' roll image.

Some people blame Elvis's movies for destroying his rebellious spirit, but Elvis had already begun to change his image by the time he resumed his movie career. Many of his fans assumed that Elvis would follow in the footsteps of James Dean and Marlon Brando and become one of Hollywood's legendary rebel heroes. Instead, he made lightweight musicals, greatly disappointing anyone who preferred the dark, sullen side of his personality. But by the time Elvis returned home from the army, Dean had been dead for five years and Brando had begun to accept traditional leading-man roles. Times had changed.

Instead of wondering what Elvis might have been, Elvis's critics should recognize what he had to offer. Most pioneer rock-'n'-roll singers did not survive the many changes the music scene went through in the 1960s; but in his own way, Elvis kept up with the times and could still find his way to the top of the charts in the 1970s. If Elvis had continued to make serious movies, such as *Flaming Star* and *Wild in the Country*, he is no more likely to have been accepted as a legitimate actor than singers Fabian, Frankie Avalon, and Pat Boone. Elvis's movies and soundtrack albums not only made him one of the highest-paid actors of the mid-1960s, they also made him a true international superstar.

CHAPTER TWELVE

BEGINNING

A NEW CAREER

There is something special about watching a man who has lost himself

find his way back home.

He sang with the kind of power people no longer associate

with rock 'n' roll singers.

He moved his body with a lack of pretension and effort that must have

made Jim Morrison green with envy.

And while most of the songs were ten or twelve years old,

he performed them as freshly as though

they were written yesterday.

JON LANDAU

ON *THE '68 COMEBACK SPECIAL*

Elvis and Priscilla are married in a brief, double-ring ceremony in Las Vegas.

By the end of the 1960s Elvis felt that his career had gone flat. He was ready to quit making movies and move on to something more challenging. The slump in his record sales and decline of his popularity, especially with teenagers, could be blamed on the kind of movies Colonel Tom Parker had negotiated for Elvis to make. The way the Colonel wrote a contract, it didn't matter if the product was any good as long as there was a substantial profit for him and his client. But one mediocre vehicle after another had strained the devotion of even Elvis's long-time supporters and failed to bring him many new fans.

At this time Elvis decided to change not only his career, but also his private life. Priscilla had been living at Graceland for several years, maintaining a low profile to keep the press away. But on May 1, 1967, Elvis brought his princess out of hiding, and he and Priscilla were married at the Aladdin Hotel in Las Vegas. It wasn't a fairy-tale wedding, but they were both very happy to be married. The double-ring ceremony lasted only eight minutes and took place in the suite of one of the Colonel's friends. Only a few of Elvis's buddies were allowed to witness the actual event (which caused some dissension among the ranks of the Memphis Mafia). Joe Esposito and Marty Lacker served as best men, and Priscilla's sister, Michelle, was the maid of honor. After the ceremony, there was a breakfast reception for 100 at the Aladdin. This event was primarily for the press. Elvis and Priscilla honeymooned in Palm Springs, and then divided their time between Graceland and their new home in Beverly Hills. On February 1, 1968, exactly nine months from the day Elvis and Priscilla were married, Lisa Marie Presley was born.

Shortly after he got married, Elvis reported to the set at MGM to begin filming *Speedway*. Although many of Elvis's biographers have suggested that he was uncomfortable about his marriage, Elvis's costar, Bill Bixby, recalls that Elvis was content and happy, even ecstatic at times. He was thinner than he had been in his last few pictures and seemed to have settled down. The time of Elvis's marriage (1967 to 1973) was also his last extended period of creativity.

Exactly nine months later, Lisa Marie Presley was born.

174

A champagne breakfast was sponsored by the couple at the Aladdin Hotel, mostly for the benefit of the press.

Elvis's marriage certificate indicated the spelling of his middle name as "Aron."

Like all young couples, at their wedding reception, Elvis and Priscilla blissfully enact the traditional wedding rituals.

The executive producer of the comeback special, Bob Finkel, won a Peabody Award for his work on the show.

Elvis belts out "If I Can Dream," the final number of Elvis—The '68 Comeback Special.

In 1968 Colonel Parker announced plans for an Elvis Presley television special on NBC. The show was planned for Christmastime, and it would be Elvis's first television appearance in eight years. Parker's plans for the special were typical of his approach to show business: get the most profit for the least amount of money and effort. He planned to keep the special simple: Elvis was to walk onto a set decorated for Christmas, introduce himself, and then humbly sing as many well-known Christmas carols as he could in an hour. For a finale Elvis was to wish everyone a happy holiday and then walk off the set. In addition to keeping production costs low, the Colonel must have expected to make at least one album of carols out of the material recorded for the special.

Fortunately for Elvis and the rest of us, the Colonel did not get his way. NBC hired Steve Binder to produce and direct Elvis's prime-time special. Binder was a pioneer in bringing rock 'n' roll to television. He created and directed *The T.A.M.I. Show*, a 1964 concert movie featuring the Supremes, Chuck Berry, James Brown, the Rolling Stones, Gerry and the Pacemakers, and Smokey Robinson and the Miracles. Binder also directed the weekly television rock 'n' roll variety show *Hullabaloo*. When he heard about the Colonel's plan for Elvis to make a conventional Christmas special, Binder flatly refused to go along with it. This placed him permanently on the Colonel's list of enemies. Binder was a fan of both Elvis and rock music, and he felt it was time for the King of Rock 'n' Roll to return from exile and reclaim his crown. Binder wanted Elvis to make a statement with this special. He wanted the show to say something about Elvis's musical roots and about the musical style he had helped develop in the 1950s.

If Binder was to succeed in turning his ideas for the special into reality, he had to secure Elvis's cooperation and trust, even if that meant encouraging Elvis to go against the Colonel. Binder knew he would have to push Elvis to challenge himself again for the first time since the early 1960s. If the special was to be any good, Elvis would have to rediscover what had made him a legend. To wake Elvis up to the fact that he really needed to start working to save his career, Binder challenged him to walk down Sunset Strip to see if there would be any reaction from the young people who hung out there. Elvis had kept himself totally isolated from the public since he was discharged from the army, and he was reluctant to expose himself to an uncontrolled crowd. But Binder prevailed, and Elvis and several members of the Memphis Mafia strolled nonchalantly down the strip. No one noticed. Elvis tried subtly to attract attention to himself, but still no one indicated that they knew who he was. If anyone on Sunset Strip recognized Elvis, they didn't seem to care. Even though the crowd on the strip was hardly a group of typical Americans, this experience helped convince Elvis that he needed a unique vehicle to put him on top again. In the battle of wills that ensued between Parker and Binder, Elvis usually sided with Binder.

Colonel Parker originally wanted the comeback special to be a quickly produced program in which Elvis packed in as many Christmas carols as possible.

Going against the Colonel's advice and wishes wasn't easy for Elvis, and Parker didn't take it well. The Colonel was at Binder's throat throughout the production. He insisted on mispronouncing the young director's name as "Bindle"; it was his way of showing his contempt and of letting Binder know that, unlike Elvis and Colonel Parker, his name was not a household word. Even though Elvis had faith in Binder's concept for the show, he never openly defied the Colonel. He would listen to Parker's demands and nod his head in agreement from time to time; but when Parker was out of the room, Elvis cooperated fully with Binder. Elvis kept assuring the young director that everything was going to be all right.

One of the production numbers in the comeback special cast Elvis as the traveling "Guitar Man."

The conflict between Binder and Parker came to a head in a disagreement over the show's finale. Parker was determined to close the special with "Silent Night," while Binder wanted to end with an original song. Binder asked the show's choral director, Earl Brown, to write a special number for the finale. Brown came up with a powerful song called "If I Can Dream," which featured a spiritual message delivered in a hip, soulful arrangement. After Brown played the song for Elvis several times, he agreed that it would make a dramatic finale. To get around the Colonel, Binder is said to have filmed Elvis singing "Silent Night," even though he had no intention of including the song in the special.

Binder's first concept for the show had Elvis playing an innocent young musician who goes out to seek his fortune only to find that the world is a wicked, sordid place. The story was to be told entirely through song and dance. Binder wanted the opening segment to take place in a brothel, but the NBC censors wouldn't allow it, so Binder decided to scrap the whole concept and come up with something else.

In its final form, the special is a series of polished production numbers designed to capture the essence of Elvis's music. There's no story line, but the musical numbers alternate with segments that were filmed before a small live audience made up mostly of women. Elvis wears a black leather jacket and pants, and his jet-black

The heartfelt intensity of Elvis's performance was apparent to all who witnessed it.

Director Steven Binder wanted the special to say something about the essence of Elvis's original rock 'n' roll music—how it had changed people's lives, how it had changed an era.

The segments that featured Elvis performing before a small studio audience perfectly captured his charisma and his electrifying effect on live crowds.

Elvis was insecure about appearing in the special, fearing the crowds would no longer be there for him. He was wrong.

hair is slightly slicked back. The effect recalls an earlier era without attempting to duplicate it. Elvis had always been an attractive man, but on this program he was radiantly handsome, and his voice had never been better. In the live segments Elvis is joined by two of his original backup musicians, D.J. Fontana and Scotty Moore. Binder wanted Elvis to sing some of his old hits and reminisce about his early career. He was supposed to talk to the audience informally, giving his opinions on modern music and telling stories about the good old days. But Elvis couldn't quite bring himself to be so open; instead, he jokes casually with Moore and Fontana and lets his music speak for him. Elvis sings many of his old songs, including "Jailhouse Rock," "Love Me Tender," and "Lawdy Miss Clawdy." But he sings with such vigor and freshness that the songs sound different, almost new. Elvis's vocal range had lowered as he got older, but he had gained confidence and control. This partly explains why the songs sound new, but Elvis was also singing with an intensity of purpose: he was making a supreme effort to regain his status as the King of Rock 'n' Roll.

Although it was recorded during the summer, the special didn't air until December 3, 1968. The show was originally titled *Singer Presents Elvis*, but it's now known as *Elvis—The '68 Comeback Special*. It was the highest-rated program for that week, and the critics praised Elvis's performance, remarking on his magic and charisma as an entertainer. The soundtrack album was received just as favorably. *The '68 Comeback Special* was a turning point in Elvis's career. Before the special, he was just a singing movie star who no longer lit any sparks. Elvis needed a challenge to push him in a new direction, and Binder had offered him that challenge. Elvis met it with an intensity he would rarely match again. *The '68 Comeback Special* is truly his finest hour.

The special marks the transition to the third phase of Elvis's career. The entertainment press may have gone back to calling him the King of Rock 'n' Roll, but Elvis never really returned to rock music. In the last part of his career, he sang everything from pop ballads to country songs, but Elvis can't be labeled a pop singer or country performer. After *The '68 Comeback Special*, Elvis transcended all labels and became simply America's Greatest Entertainer.

Elvis realized that this television special represented a turning point in his career. He met the challenge with an intensity he would rarely possess again.

CHAPTER THIRTEEN

LIVE ONSTAGE

At 9:15 Elvis appeared, materialized,

in a white suit of lights, shining with golden appliques,

the shirt front slashed to show his chest.

Around his shoulders was a cape lined in a cloth of gold,

its collar faced with scarlet.

It was anything you wanted to call it, gaudy,

vulgar, magnificent.

DONNA MUIR

1972

Three years in Elvis's career stand out as turning points: 1956, 1960, and 1969. Each of these years marked the beginning of a new image and a new sound for Elvis. In 1956 Elvis began to rock 'n' roll; his music was new and his performing style was dangerous. In 1960 Elvis the Pelvis became Elvis the singing movie star; he appealed to a wider audience and became tops at the box office. In 1969 Elvis began to distance himself from his movie musicals and became an international pop star; his songs topped the charts and his dazzling live performances earned him the title of "World's Greatest Entertainer."

Back in the fall of 1967, Elvis had already begun to move away from the style of his soundtrack albums. Under the direction of RCA record producer Felton Jarvis, Elvis had recorded two country rock songs: "Big Boss Man," released in 1967, and "Guitar Man," released in January 1968. These two singles were the forerunners of the songs that would once more bring Elvis success on the charts in the late 1960s and early 1970s. During that same session Elvis also recorded "High Heel Sneakers," "You Don't Know Me," "Too Much," and "U.S. Male."

In 1968 RCA had released the single "If I Can Dream," the song Elvis sang at the end of his 1968 comeback special. By January 1969 it had reached number 12 on the pop listings, proving that Elvis's recordings could once again make it to the charts. "If I Can Dream" became Elvis's biggest single since 1965. The soundtrack album from the special, titled simply *Elvis*, reached number eight on the pop album charts.

The recordings Elvis made with Felton Jarvis and the success of his television special inspired Elvis to record more contemporary material, and a ten-day recording session was booked for January 1969. Instead of using RCA's recording studio in Nashville, Elvis used American Sound Studios, a small independent studio in Memphis. Elvis's decision to use a small recording studio was not unusual. Independent studios provided a relaxed atmosphere and conscientious attention to detail that were not always available at larger recording studios. American Sound Studios had gained a reputation as one of the most successful independent studios in the industry. Chips Moman, one of the owners who also served as an engineer, was Elvis's producer. He had experience working with chart-topping singers of many different kinds of music. The studio also had a great house band made up of musicians who were well-versed in

In 1956 Elvis exploded onto the national scene with a revolutionary musical sound and a provocative performance style. Compared to the rest of the Eisenhower Era, Elvis was dangerous.

In 1960 the Colonel helped Elvis to take advantage of his stint in the army to present a new, more mature image to the public. Elvis the Pelvis became Elvis the movie star.

In 1969 Elvis Presley—the King of Rock 'n' Roll—once again burst onto the entertainment scene to reclaim his crown from younger pretenders to the throne.

In 1969, Elvis returned to the charts by recording contemporary material by talented young songwriters instead of relying solely on the music from his movie soundtracks.

country music, rhythm and blues, and rock 'n' roll. Elvis probably felt right at home at American Sound Studios; the place had a rough, down-home feel that must have reminded him of Sun Studios in the 1950s.

Chips Moman was to be a big influence on Elvis; he helped Elvis develop the style and sound he would use for the rest of his career. The house band was also on the same wavelength as Elvis. They shared his Southern roots, had been influenced by him in the 1950s, and were his musical heirs. They seemed to fully understand the direction his music was taking. The style Elvis worked out with Chips Moman and the band wasn't straightforward rock 'n' roll, and it wasn't traditional country or rhythm and blues. It took something from all these kinds of music, but it was unique. No song demonstrates this more clearly than "Suspicious Minds," with its seemingly endless crescendos and all-encompassing sound. The way Elvis delivers this song captures the essence of his new musical style.

Elvis had planned to record for ten days during January 1969, but he had laryngitis and was able to work for only six days. In spite of this, the session was so successful that Elvis returned to American Sound Studios for five more days of recording the following month. During these two recording sessions Elvis did some of the best work of his career. He recorded three top-10 singles: "Suspicious Minds," "Don't Cry Daddy," and "In the Ghetto," and a lot of other great material, including "Kentucky Rain," "Only the Strong Survive," and "I'm Movin' On." The recordings made during these sessions were released on two albums: *From Elvis in Memphis* and *From Memphis to Vegas/From Vegas to Memphis*.

The 36 tracks recorded at American Sound Studios covered a wide range of music—from country tunes to contemporary soul. The best songs didn't come from RCA's own music publisher, Hill and Range, but from young, independent songwriters, including Mark James, Mac Davis, and the team of Eddie Rabbit and Dick Heard. It's unlikely that Colonel Parker and Freddie Bienstock of Hill and Range were pleased by Elvis's decision to record material they didn't control. When Elvis recorded songs by songwriters who were not under contract to Hill and Range or songs that had not been acquired by Elvis Presley Music, Elvis and his management team did not receive any publishing royalties. The Colonel and Bienstock are said to have been particularly

When Elvis decided to take a different direction in his career by recording new material at a studio away from RCA's facilities in Nashville, he chose American Sound Studios in his hometown of Memphis.

upset about Elvis's determination to record "Suspicious Minds" since Chips Moman owned the publishing rights to it. Supposedly, Parker tried to pressure Moman into giving him a piece of the rights, but Moman refused. Parker even threatened to persuade RCA not to release the song if Elvis and Moman went ahead and recorded it against his wishes. But the matter was quickly settled when an RCA executive arrived in Memphis and realized the song had the potential to become a hit. Elvis was given the go-ahead to record "Suspicious Minds," and RCA guaranteed that it would be released.

Part of Elvis's 1968 comeback special had been recorded before a live audience, and although Elvis had not performed on stage since 1961, it was clear that he hadn't forgotten any of his old tricks. He had no trouble winning over the audience. The success of these live segments encouraged Elvis to return to the stage, and it wasn't long before he got a spectacular offer. In the early summer of 1969 Elvis was invited to play the newly opened International Hotel in Las Vegas. The main room of the hotel had not been opened, and Elvis was asked to do the honors. But the Colonel decided that Elvis shouldn't take the chance of making his comeback on a brand-new and untested stage, so Barbra Streisand was booked to open the main room of the

International in July, and Elvis was scheduled for August. According to his contract, the marquee would read simply "Elvis." Although reports on the exact amount of his salary vary widely, Elvis was paid half a million dollars for four weeks. He had played Las Vegas only once before, at the New Frontier Hotel in April 1956, not long after he had begun performing outside the South. That show had bombed, and Elvis still felt the sting of that disappointing failure. He was understandably nervous about making his comeback in Las Vegas.

On opening night at the International, Elvis wore a modified karate suit made especially for him out of black mohair.

For his return to live performing, Elvis chose not to re-create his earlier image or sound. His music was no longer as simple as it had been in the early 1960s, and his Las Vegas act was on a much larger scale than his earlier shows. Elvis's first band had consisted of a guitarist, a bass player, and a drummer. For his Las Vegas performances, Elvis was joined on stage by the Imperials (a pop/gospel quartet), the Sweet Inspirations (a female backup trio), a rock band, and a 35-piece orchestra. The members of the rock band included well-known Southern blues guitarist James Burton, drummer Ronnie Tutt, bassist Jerry Scheff, keyboard player Larry Muhoberack, and guitarists/vocalists John Wilkinson and Charlie Hodge. (Hodge had been part of the Memphis Mafia since the days when he and Elvis were in the army together.) The room at the International was enormous, and Elvis needed an orchestra to fill the place with sound, but he also needed this large entourage to fulfill his image as the World's Greatest Entertainer.

Elvis was extremely nervous about his upcoming live performances. There had only been time for a few rehearsals before the opening, and there had been no opportunity for Elvis to work out the kinks in his act before a live audience—all of which must have added to his anxiety. But if Elvis was nervous, Colonel Parker was in his element, and he was busy promoting Elvis all over Las Vegas. He rented every available billboard and took out full-page ads in the local and trade papers. The lobby of the International was filled with Elvis Presley souvenirs—T-shirts, straw boaters, records, and even stuffed animals. The Colonel made sure that Elvis's return to the stage would be the show-business event of the year. Kirk Kerkorian, the owner of the International at that time, planned to send his own plane to New York to fly in the rock-music press for opening night. The list of celebrities planning to attend Elvis's opening included Cary Grant, Pat Boone, Fats Domino, Wayne Newton, Dick Clark, Ann-Margret, George Hamilton, Angie Dickinson, and Henry Mancini. Elvis even invited Sam Phillips, the man who had helped him develop his raw talent into a unique musical style.

Vernon Presley beams proudly as Elvis sets new attendance records at the International Hotel.

Elvis and Priscilla greet well-wishers backstage during his 1969 Las Vegas engagement.

On July 31, 1969, Elvis performed in front of a sold-out crowd of 2,000 people. As his band pounded out "Baby, I Don't Care," Elvis walked on stage. There was no emcee to introduce him. He grabbed the microphone, struck a familiar pose from the past, and snapped his leg back and forth almost imperceptibly. The crowd roared uncontrollably, jumping from their chairs to give him a standing ovation before he had sung one note. The audience whistled, applauded furiously, and pounded on the tables; some people stood on their chairs. When the ovation began to subside, Elvis launched into "Blue Suede Shoes" with such fury that it seemed as though his life depended on it. Maybe he thought it did.

Elvis looked unbelievably handsome that night. He was dressed in a modified karate suit made specially for him out of black mohair. He was thinner than he had been in his last few films, and his blue-black hair reached down past his collar. Elvis's sideburns were the longest they had been since the 1950s. Never one to take himself too seriously, Elvis joked with the crowd about the old days and the old songs. At one

Elvis looked incredibly handsome during his comeback to live performances at the International Hotel in August of 1969.

point he decided to dedicate his next number to the audience and the staff at the International: "This is the only song I could think of that really expresses my feeling toward the audience," he said in all earnestness; then he burst into "Hound Dog." Elvis closed his act with "What'd I Say" from *Viva Las Vegas*, and again the crowd gave him a standing ovation. Elvis came back for an encore and sang the song he would close every show with for the rest of his career: "Can't Help Falling in Love."

Las Vegas showgirl Pat Gill offers Elvis her congratulations.

Backstage after the performance, many celebrities and well wishers were on hand to congratulate Elvis on his successful return to live performing. In her account of her life with Elvis, Priscilla Presley relates a touching story about Colonel Parker. At this moment of great personal and professional triumph for his one and only client, the Colonel pushed his way backstage with tears welling up in his eyes. Elvis emerged from his dressing room, and the two men embraced, too overcome with emotion to say anything. There have been many stories about Colonel Tom Parker that show him in a less-than-favorable light, but no story better reveals the complexity of the relationship between singer and manager.

Most members of the rock 'n' roll press, many of whom were teenagers when Elvis began his career, were ecstatic about his return to the stage and expressed their enthusiasm in glowing reviews. *Rolling Stone* magazine declared Elvis to be supernatural; *Variety* proclaimed him a superstar; and *Newsweek* praised him for his staying power. Elvis was once more the King of Rock 'n' Roll.

The day after Elvis's opening night, the Colonel sat down with the general manager of the International to discuss the enormous success of the performance. The hotel offered Elvis a five-year contract to play two months a' year—February and August—at a salary of one million dollars per year. In his usual flamboyant style, the Colonel took out a pen and began scribbling specific terms on the red tablecloth. When he finished, he asked the general manager to sign the cloth to close the deal. Although the "red tablecloth deal" has become a show business legend, many people have criticized Parker for locking Elvis into a long-term contract that didn't take inflation into account. Had he negotiated contracts with the hotel on a year-by-year basis, the Colonel and Elvis probably would have made a lot more money.

Elvis's jumpsuits, accented with studs and gems, often featured matching capes.

Six months after his first Las Vegas show, Elvis returned to the International for another month of sold-out performances. During this engagement Elvis began to wear a jumpsuit on stage. Bill Belew, who had designed the black leather outfit Elvis wore during his 1968 comeback special, designed a white jumpsuit that was slashed down the front to show off Elvis's chest, fitted closely at the waist, and belled out at the legs, which was the fashion of the day. The costume's high collar was inset with semiprecious jewels, and Elvis wore gold and diamond rings on the fingers of both hands. A macramé karate belt made of gold- and pearl-colored strands accentuated his slender waist. Compared with the costumes Elvis wore during his later Las Vegas appearances and tours, this first jumpsuit was rather conservative. Over the years, Elvis's costumes became more and more elaborate, and the jumpsuits were often accompanied by waist-length or even floor-length capes. According to friends and family members, the gems, gold chains, and rivets that decorated these costumes were real and could weigh as much as 30 pounds. Simply standing up in such a heavy costume must have been physically exhausting, but Elvis somehow managed to move quickly and gracefully onstage under hot lights. His costumes, particularly the belts, were emblazoned with certain symbols that had significance for Elvis such as eagles, karate symbols, tigers, and sundials. His fans refer to Elvis's costumes by name: the Mexican Sundial, the King of Spades, the Rainbow Swirl, the American Eagle, the Red Flower, the Gypsy, and the Dragon. They identify Elvis's different tours and appearances by the costumes he wore.

Dean Martin attended Elvis's second Las Vegas engagement on opening night, and Elvis sang "Everybody Loves Somebody Sometime" as a tribute to Martin, whom he had always admired. The song fit right in with Elvis's repertoire, which included everything from contemporary country songs to rock ballads. Elvis used his old material in only a few key places during the show and sometimes sang his old songs arranged in a medley. He was determined not to rest on his laurels, so he included contemporary material as well as the new sound he had developed with Chips Moman at the American Sound Studios.

Elvis dressed as flamboyantly in his everyday life as he did on stage.

Elvis's jumpsuits seemed to become more elaborate every year.

Elvis's show was not just a nostalgia act, although the success of his comeback was probably enhanced by the revival of 1950s music that began in the late 1960s. Many performers who had helped develop the rock 'n' roll sound and attitude reaped the benefits of this renewed interest in the roots of rock music. Bill Haley and the Comets, Chuck Berry, and Jerry Lee Lewis were touring once again and attracting large crowds. Elvis's success not only benefited from the rock-nostalgia craze; it also undoubtedly influenced it. But Elvis was careful to keep his own material new and varied. He didn't identify himself with the rock 'n' roll revival, and his show was never considered merely an oldies act.

Following his success in Las Vegas, Elvis took his act on tour. For Elvis's first show on the road, Colonel Parker arranged for him to appear at the Houston Astrodome for a week in conjunction with the Texas Livestock Show. The Astrodome seats 44,500 people, and the Colonel probably figured that since only the World's Greatest Entertainer could hope to sell out such a huge arena, Elvis's legendary status would be assured if he could fill the Astrodome. Texas had always been good to Elvis. In 1955 East Texas had been the scene of a great surge of Elvis-mania, which helped boost his early career. To return this kindness, and perhaps to ensure a sellout, the tickets for Elvis's engagement at the Astrodome were greatly reduced in price, with some seats selling for as little as one dollar.

Colonel Parker was in his element in Las Vegas, where he could promote his boy in the carnival-like atmosphere to which Parker was accustomed.

Even though Elvis must have been pretty self-confident after his recent Vegas victories, he was overwhelmed by the size of the Astrodome and the thought of having to please 44,500 people at once. He said that he felt like the place was an ocean, and he worried about not being as dynamic in such a vast arena as he had been in Las Vegas. His fears proved unfounded; the Astrodome sold out each night of his engagement, and the local music critics raved about his personal charisma and his exciting act. For the first time since the 1950s, Elvis was mobbed after one of his shows. His limousine had been parked by the stage door so Elvis could make a rapid getaway, but the fans were able to reach the car too quickly. They surrounded the vehicle, trying to give their idol flowers and gifts and wanting to touch him.

After the success in Houston, Elvis continued to tour, and his schedule was grueling. He was usually on the road for several weeks out of each month in addition to playing Las Vegas in February and August. By 1971 Elvis was on the road for three weeks at a time, taking no days off and doing two shows on Saturday and Sunday. Then he'd rest for a few weeks and then go back on tour. Elvis usually played one-night stands, and since almost every performance was scheduled for a different arena, Elvis and his entourage would usually arrive in a city and depart again in less than 24 hours. This demanding schedule took its toll in terms of Elvis's desire to update or change the material in his act, and eventually his performances became standardized. Despite this, Elvis's concerts were almost always sold out.

Elvis's return to concert performing probably contributed to the problems that eventually ended his marriage. Being on tour meant being away from Graceland most of the time, and he saw very little of Priscilla and his daughter. The horrendous pace of performing in a different city every night made traveling with a family too difficult. (Elvis also enforced a no-wives rule for the rest of his entourage while they were on the road.) In early 1972 Priscilla decided she could no longer live with Elvis, and Elvis sued for divorce the following August. Elvis's lawyer released a succinct statement about the divorce: "Elvis has been spending six months a year on the road, which put a tremendous strain on the marriage." In October 1973 the couple were officially divorced, but it was an amicable split. They held hands during the divorce proceedings and walked out of the courtroom arm in arm.

Elvis and Priscilla were divorced in October of 1973. The split was an amicable one, with the couple walking out of the courtroom arm in arm. Elvis said of Priscilla, "She was one of the few girls who was interested in me for me alone."

After the divorce, Priscilla pursued her own interests. She owned and operated a fashionable boutique in Beverly Hills for a short time, and then became involved in acting.

Elvis meets the press in New York before his sold-out series of concerts at Madison Square Garden.

In June 1972 Elvis played Madison Square Garden—the first time he'd ever performed live in New York. All four shows at the Garden quickly sold out, but Elvis and his management team were afraid that the sophisticated New York critics wouldn't like his Las Vegas style. Elvis was decked out in one of his bejeweled jumpsuits on opening night. The outfit included a gold-lined cape and a gigantic belt emblazoned with "World Champion Entertainer"—just in case the critics didn't know who was performing. Throughout the show, particularly while he was singing his old songs, Elvis maintained an ironic distance from his audience. Sometimes he couldn't resist joking about his former image. At the beginning of "Hound Dog," for example, Elvis dramatically dropped down to one knee and then said, "Oh, excuse me," before switching to the other knee.

During his New York engagement Elvis appeared to be in top physical condition. His voice was strong and clear, and he sang a variety of old and new songs with drama and flair. Most of the New York critics were enthusiastic. RCA recorded all four shows at the Garden for an album to be called *Elvis as Recorded at Madison Square Garden*. The record company mixed the songs, pressed the records, and had the albums in stores in less than two weeks.

A typical Elvis Presley concert of the 1970s was more like a ceremony than a performance by an entertainer. Accompanied by Richard Strauss's "Also sprach Zarathustra," popularly known as the "Theme from *2001*," Elvis would charge into the spotlight as though propelled by some supernatural force. His onstage moves incorporated karate kicks and tai-chi arabesques as well as heroic stances and dramatic postures. In the 1950s Elvis's performances had always been sensuous—with bumps and grinds calculated to illicit screams and hysterics from the audience. In the 1970s this aspect of his performance changed significantly. Elvis mocked his 1950s sex-symbol image with exaggerated pelvic thrusts, grandiose poses and jokes about the old days.

While he performed, Elvis would often wipe the sweat from his brow and then throw the towel into the audience. This gesture was so popular with his audiences that dozens of white towels were kept just offstage so that Elvis could throw them into the audience at frequent intervals. But Elvis wasn't the only one throwing things during his

There were two rituals that female fans enjoyed at all of Elvis's concerts—kissing the King and grabbing for those sweat-soaked towels.

196

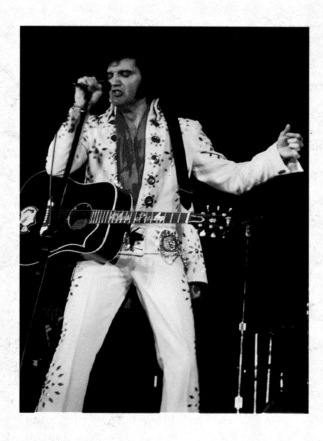

Elvis was dynamic in Las Vegas during the early 1970s (top), but his successful engagement at Madison Square Garden in June of 1972 (bottom) was probably the highpoint of this phase of his career.

Though Elvis made no more fictional films after 1969, he was the focus of two documentaries. The first, Elvis: That's the Way It Is, *chronicled his 1970 Las Vegas engagement.*

performances. In Las Vegas, women in the audience would throw their underwear and sometimes their room keys onstage. Each time Elvis played the International, the hotel stocked its restrooms with fresh undergarments. While the practice of throwing underwear is not unique to Las Vegas, it's widely accepted there, and this ritual is still enacted when pop singers Tom Jones and Englebert Humperdinck perform there.

Elvis always opened his concerts with an old-fashioned Vegas-style comedian, even when he was on the road. Many rock music fans were appalled by this. If they had to listen to a stand-up comic, they would have preferred a hip new comedian with socially relevant material. When Elvis played Madison Square Garden, the opening comic was actually booed off the stage by the fans, who had come to see Elvis and Elvis only. But his opening act was part of Elvis's heritage from the 1950s. Even when he was on the cutting edge of rock 'n' roll back in 1956 and 1957, Elvis had always toured with an oddball assortment of vaudeville acts—booked, no doubt, by the Colonel. There were always a couple of comedians who specialized in one-liners and nightclub humor. So when Elvis returned to the stage, he and the Colonel kept the same kind of opening act. Not only were they accustomed to this kind of show business humor, but it also went over well in Vegas. Sammy Shore opened for Elvis in the early 1970s, and Jackie Kahane did the honors after 1972.

It was Kahane's responsibility to announce, "Ladies and gentlemen, Elvis has left the building." This signaled the close of each concert. Elvis rarely performed an encore, but the audience usually remained in their seats after the final number, hoping Elvis would respond to the thunderous applause and return for one last song. But to avoid problems with overzealous fans, Elvis would usually run backstage immediately after his last song, often while the band was still playing, and dash into a car waiting at the stage door. Kahane's announcement let the audience know that it was truly time to leave.

Although Elvis's enormous popularity forced him to live secluded from the public, his performances gave the illusion of intimacy. His rapport with the audience was based on treating them like old friends or an extended family. There was always a great deal of interaction between Elvis and members of the audience. They would throw things to him, and he would throw towels back to them. Elvis would kiss and hug women in the audience or hold their hands. Women would line up just below the stage, waiting to be blessed by the King's touch. The audience expected Elvis to sing certain songs, perform specific moves, and tell familiar stories; and he always fulfilled their expectations. An outsider might have expected Elvis's act to go stale by the mid-1970s, but he was still giving his faithful audience what they had come to see. They wouldn't have wanted his show to be any different.

Elvis had always had an uncanny instinct for knowing what his fans wanted. During the early part of his career, when audiences were hysterical over his gyrations, they came to Elvis's concerts hoping he would take his performance to new heights of intensity. Sensing this, Elvis would tease them with a few hip and leg movements, the audience would scream louder, and then he would really cut loose. Elvis usually singled out several members of the audience and directed his looks and gestures specifically to them. The bond that formed between performer and audience was strong, and Elvis's fans were unusually loyal and demonstrative throughout his life. The special bond between Elvis and his fans sustained his popularity long after critics lost interest in his career.

MGM produced two documentaries that capture Elvis's live performances. *Elvis, That's the Way It Is* is a feature-length movie built around Elvis's August 1970 engagement in Las Vegas. About half of the movie is from a performance in the main room of the International Hotel. The segment in which Elvis sings "Mystery Train" and "Tiger Man" was filmed at a concert in Phoenix. The rest of the movie documents the excitement Elvis generated as a performer. Elvis is shown in rehearsal for the show, whipping his band into shape and mastering new material for the act. There are shots of the massive promotional buildup in Las Vegas, and also footage from an Elvis Presley convention in Luxembourg.

As seen in Elvis: That's the Way It Is, *Elvis worked hard during rehearsal for his Las Vegas engagement.*

Elvis, That's the Way It Is was directed by Denis Sanders, who won an Oscar for Best Documentary for his film *Czechoslovakia, 1968*. Expert cinematographer Lucien Ballard caught the excitement of Elvis's performance on stage with eight Panavision cameras. The film was released on November 11, 1970, to good reviews. The *Hollywood*

Elvis as seen in Andrew Solt's free-wheeling documentary This Is Elvis.

Reporter remarked that Elvis was probably the only entertainer alive who could draw enough people to a theater to make a documentary pay off. The film also introduced Elvis as a live performer to an audience who was too young to remember him in performance in the 1950s and only knew Elvis from his movies.

In 1972 MGM released another feature-length Elvis documentary, which had been shot in the spring of that year. *Elvis on Tour* focuses on his road show during a 15-city tour. This film captures the final phase of Elvis's career at its highest point. It was produced by Pierre Adidge and Robert Abel, who had won critical acclaim for their rock documentary *Joe Cocker: Mad Dogs and Englishmen*. Some of the editing was supervised by Martin Scorsese, who also worked on editing *Woodstock*. Andrew Solt is credited with doing research for *Elvis on Tour*. He later coproduced the free-wheeling documentary *This Is Elvis* as well as *Imagine*, a film about John Lennon. *Elvis on Tour* won a Golden Globe award for the Best Documentary of 1972; it's the only Elvis Presley movie to be honored with an award of any kind.

In January 1973 Elvis returned to television with a spectacular special, *Elvis: Aloha from Hawaii*. The show was a benefit for cancer research, and all the proceeds from the concert went to the Kui Lee Cancer Fund. Elvis's performance at the Honolulu International Center Arena was broadcast live via the Intelsat IV communications satellite to Japan, South Korea, the Philippines, New Zealand, Australia, Thailand, South Vietnam, and other countries in the Far East. Two days later a taped replay was aired in Europe, and in April the special was rebroadcast on American television. Over one-and-a-half billion people eventually watched this one performance. Dressed in a trademark jumpsuit with matching cape, Elvis sang new material and well-known hit songs. By the end of the show he was so caught up in the enthusiasm of the audience and the magnitude of the event that he hurled his cape, which was worth several thousand dollars, into the audience.

Elvis on Tour, *which chronicled the King's whirlwind road show across 15 cities in the spring of 1972, won a Golden Globe as Best Documentary.*

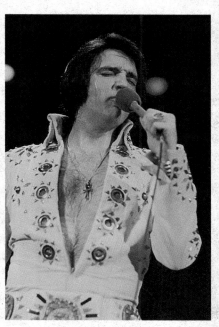

Most fans who remember Elvis's concerts from the 1970s claim that the intimacy of his performances and his charisma could never be captured on film.

The television special Elvis: Aloha from Hawaii *marked another milestone in Elvis's career. Over one and a half billion people from around the world watched the broadcast.*

In a typically generous gesture, Elvis donated the proceeds from the Aloha from Hawaii *concert to the Kuiokalani Lee Cancer Fund.*

By the time of the Hawaii special, Elvis had developed a standard format for his act from which he never varied; but his repertoire of songs continued to change. His songs often seemed to tell his audience about what was going on in his life. Elvis had always been a deeply religious man, and when he sang "How Great Thou Art," Elvis's fans knew he really meant what he was singing. A live recording of the song from the 1974 album *Elvis Recorded Live on Stage in Memphis* won a Grammy Award for Best Inspirational Performance. Around 1972, when Elvis's marriage was falling apart, he brought two songs into his repertoire that reflected the trials and tribulations of his love life: "Always on My Mind" and "You Gave Me a Mountain." Elvis also began to sing "My Way," which Paul Anka had originally written for Frank Sinatra. The song became a personal anthem for Elvis; it seemed musically to justify his eccentric lifestyle and his larger-than-life image. The lyrics are about a man looking back on his life as death draws near. A recording of Elvis's moving version of this song was not released until June 1977, just two months before his death.

Rumor has it that some lucky television viewers in Communist China were able to pick up Elvis: Aloha from Hawaii.

In 1971 country songwriter Mickey Newbury put together a unique arrangement of three nineteenth-century songs, which he recorded and released as "An American Trilogy." Elvis heard the record and quickly adopted the medley for his act. "An American Trilogy" has become so closely associated with Elvis that it's hard to imagine anyone else performing it. When Elvis did the number, which combines "Dixie," "The Battle Hymn of the Republic," and the spiritual "All My Trials," it was a show stopper. The medley reflects Elvis's patriotism, his religious convictions, and his deep affection for his native South. Elvis's passionate interpretation of the piece could stir the souls of even his strongest detractors.

The years 1969 through 1973 had been an incredibly creative time for Elvis. He had returned to performing live and developed a new sound and a new image that completely replaced the singing-movie-star image that he had never felt really matched his talents. The new Elvis, dressed in gold and jewels, was truly the King of Rock 'n' Roll. This flamboyant image of Elvis is remembered and copied today by hundreds of Elvis impersonators, because although Elvis had always been a legendary performer to his fans, everyone who saw Elvis live onstage came to think of him as an immortal superstar.

CHAPTER FOURTEEN

LIFE AT COURT

Elvis was a country boy,

but the way they had him living, they never turned off

the air conditioning.

Took away all the good air.

You get sick from that.

JAMES BROWN

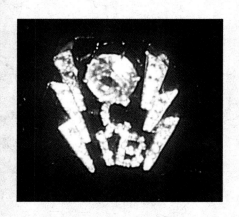

Elvis's TCB insignia—"Taking Care of Business."

Elvis lived the life of rock 'n' roll royalty. He was the King—adored by his fans, wealthy almost beyond belief, and dressed in jewels and flowing capes. Elvis enjoyed the privileges and pleasures of his exalted position, but his eccentric and secluded lifestyle eventually led to abuse of his position and of himself.

Like all kings, Elvis had his court. The entertainment press called this group of close friends, business associates, and employees the "Memphis Mafia." They not only worked for Elvis but they also kept him entertained. Elvis, the Colonel, and Vernon Presley never paid the members of the Mafia very high wages, but Elvis loaned them money for down payments on houses and gave them automobiles, motorcycles, trucks, jewelry, guns, and other expensive gifts. Most of the Memphis Mafia worked for Elvis out of friendship, not for the money, and many of the men were so close to him that they lived at Graceland from time to time.

Over the years the faces in the group changed, but a few remained with Elvis for much of his career. The most prominent members of the court include Red and Sonny West (who were cousins), Marty Lacker, Joe Esposito, George Klein, Jerry Schilling, Charlie Hodge, Gene Smith (Elvis's cousin), Lamar Fike, and Alan Fortas. Some members of the Memphis Mafia didn't work for Elvis exclusively and had their own careers. George Klein was a Memphis disc jockey for most of his life. Red West, who started hanging out with Elvis around 1955, worked as a stunt man in Hollywood. In addition to doing stunt work in most of Elvis's movies, he was in the movie *Spartacus* and worked on several television series. West also wrote songs for Elvis and other singers, including Ricky Nelson, Pat Boone, and Johnny Rivers.

King Elvis and his royal court had their own coat of arms: a lightning bolt combined with the initials TCB. Elvis designed the insignia to symbolize the code of behavior he wanted his entourage to live by. TCB stands for "taking care of business," and the lightning bolt represents speed; so Elvis's coat of arms means "taking care of business in a flash." The King liked everything to be done quickly and efficiently. Elvis had charms made up with this insignia for each member of the Memphis Mafia, and many of the men wore them on chains around their necks. Elvis also had TLC charms made up for the wives and girlfriends of his favorite companions. TLC stands for "tender loving care."

During the 1960s, members of the Memphis Mafia would join Elvis on location while he was making movies. Some of the men had bit parts, but their main job was to keep Elvis company. While he was shooting a movie in Hollywood, Elvis and his entourage lived in a Bel Air mansion that had once belonged to the Shah of Iran. The house was the scene of many late-night parties, which were often attended by a host of Hollywood starlets.

When Elvis first came to Hollywood, he organized a football team to relieve the tedium of movie production. Elvis and his court were joined on the football field by Kent McCord, Ty Hardin, Pat Boone, Robert Conrad, Gary Lockwood, and Ricky Nelson. As time went on, Elvis took up more expensive hobbies to fill his time in Hollywood. On one shopping spree while he was making *Tickle Me*, Elvis bought all of his friends motorcycles so they could go riding together. Another time, Elvis had his men go to three photo shops and buy out all their flashbulbs. Then they dumped the bulbs in a swimming pool and shot them with BB guns. When a bulb was hit, it would explode and sink. After three nights of shooting, it took two days to clean the pool.

Elvis, who loved football, organized teams in both Hollywood and Memphis.

Toward the end of his movie career, when Elvis had become bored with making movies, his antics and practical jokes got wilder and more elaborate. At times, the kidding around seemed to take precedence over acting. Pie fights were common, and on the set of *Easy Come, Easy Go,* director John Rich often objected to Elvis's constant fooling around. During one scene Elvis kept bursting into laughter every time he looked at Red or Sonny West, blowing his lines in take after take. Rich lost his temper and ordered everyone off the set, but Elvis stepped in and set Rich straight. "We're doing these movies because it's supposed to be fun, nothing more," he told the director. "When they cease to be fun, then we'll cease to do them." But during the filming of *Clambake,* Elvis's gang caused so much confusion on the set that when production on **his next movie, *Stay Away, Joe,* began, a memo came down from the MGM executive offices warning Elvis and the Memphis Mafia that rowdy behavior would not be tolerated.**

Elvis insisted on being treated as roughly as any other team member. Shortly after being discharged from the army, Elvis broke his little finger in a touch football game with some friends in Memphis.

Karate was an interest Elvis picked up while in the army. He and the members of the Memphis Mafia not only practiced the sport but also enjoyed watching tournaments.

Elvis and Red West often practiced karate moves together. Red, who had been with Elvis since about 1955, was perhaps his closest friend.

207

Whatever hobby or toy Elvis became interested in, he also bought in quantity for his buddy-bodyguards. In 1975 Elvis bought the whole gang three-wheeled cycles with Volkswagen-powered engines.

When Elvis wasn't working on a movie, he and his buddy bodyguards would retreat behind the gates of Graceland. Occasionally late at night when they were sure most people were asleep, they would venture out into Memphis to seek entertainment or ride their motorcycles. Since Elvis's persistent fans prevented him from going out during normal hours, he would often rent the Malco or the Memphian movie theater from midnight to dawn. Elvis, his friends, and their guests would stay up all night watching the latest movies as well as older films. Sometimes Elvis enjoyed seeing his own movies; but he never watched *Jailhouse Rock* because his leading lady, Judy Tyler, had been killed, or *Loving You*, because of his mother's brief appearance in the movie. Before midnight movies at the Malco became his passion, Elvis would also rent amusement parks or roller skating rinks after-hours for the entertainment of his friends.

When Elvis first became a national singing sensation, he enjoyed the adoring fans who followed him around or waited for him in front of his house. On his first visit to Hollywood, Elvis and his buddies cruised up and down Hollywood Boulevard, inciting his fans to follow their car. They'd pull up to a stoplight and Elvis would roll down his car window, take off his sunglasses, and yell to the girls standing on the corner. When the light changed, Elvis and company would take off again, leaving a crowd of people screaming hysterically in the middle of the intersection or chasing their car down the street.

But it wasn't long before Elvis's fans became unmanageable. He was mobbed, pushed down, and sometimes stripped bare by crowds of adoring admirers. Elvis couldn't sightsee, eat in a restaurant, or enjoy himself in public without his fans besieging him. By the time Elvis was discharged from the army, he had begun living as a recluse— secluding himself at Graceland or in his home in California. This isolation, coupled with the boredom that came between projects and the privileges that came with stardom, eventually led Elvis to indulge in several self-destructive habits. Things got even worse after he began spending much of his time on the road. His worst problem was obviously his dependence on prescription drugs, which altered his behavior and personality. According to members of the Memphis Mafia, Elvis had begun using amphetamines in the 1960s to keep his weight down. To counteract the amphetamines, Elvis and his court (who always indulged in whatever Elvis was doing) began taking sleeping pills. During the 1970s, when Elvis was touring on a debilitating schedule of one-nighters, he was also taking medication for severe pain. These drugs eventually left Elvis in a state of mental limbo. Members of the Memphis Mafia disagree about how many drugs Elvis took, but the fact remains that he took more than his body could withstand. His drug abuse not only brought on a decline in his career, but it also led to his death.

By 1957, Elvis could not appear in public without being mobbed, shoved around, or stripped bare by adoring fans.

Elvis's drug problem was the result of prescription drugs, some of which were administered for actual health problems: he had back pain, digestive troubles, and many eye afflictions, including glaucoma. These conditions put Elvis in the hospital several times between 1973 and his death four years later. He was also hospitalized for throat ailments, pleurisy, and hypertension. Ironically, Elvis rarely indulged in alcohol and often spoke out against taking illegal drugs.

While the obvious decline in the quality of Elvis's records after the early 1970s is undoubtedly the result of his self-destructive lifestyle, RCA was also partly responsible. No matter how often Elvis recorded material (and some years he didn't enter a recording studio at all), RCA released three albums every year. The record company was able to do this by issuing live albums from concerts and Las Vegas appearances and by repackaging songs from earlier albums.

The price of fame: The bars on the fence in this photo seem to symbolize the prison-like existence that Elvis led.

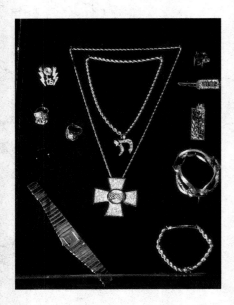

The crown jewels: A collection of the King's jewelry is on display at Graceland.

Because of his wealth and position, Elvis could indulge himself to excess. How much he overindulged his bad habits has been exaggerated because Elvis's kingly excesses have become part of his legend. All kinds of outrageous statements have been made about Elvis's eating habits. He was a lifelong fan of junk food and Southern-style cooking. As early as 1955, when he was an up-and-coming country singer, articles about Elvis often mentioned that he liked to down several cheeseburgers at one sitting. An article in *Esquire* magazine in the late 1960s took a sarcastic but lighthearted tone when describing Elvis's favorite snack of peanut butter and mashed-banana sandwiches washed down with several Pepsis. After Elvis's death, these reports began to seem more sinister. They suggest that Elvis was out of control and that his eating habits and weight problems were somehow related to his drug abuse. However, these attempts at armchair psychology don't take into account the fact that Elvis ate the same way all his life; his eating habits only became a health problem when he got older and didn't exercise.

Elvis loved traditional Southern-style cooking, which features a lot of meat and rich, fried food. Reporters and magazine writers who were unfamiliar with Southern cooking felt that Elvis's eating habits were peculiar, although many people in the South enjoy the same foods. Writers told tall tales about Elvis eating so many Spanish omelettes that he created an egg shortage in Tennessee. It was also said that in one night he once ate 30 cups of yogurt, eight honeydew melons, and $100 worth of ice cream bars. While Elvis sometimes went on eating binges, particularly during his time off between projects, the stories about binges on foods such as bacon, ice cream, cheeseburgers, and pizza have been repeated so often that it seems as though Elvis ate that much every day. Although it's true that Elvis had many unhealthy eating habits and gained a great deal of weight, the stories about what he ate are often wildly exaggerated. It's as though Elvis's larger-than-life image, particularly during the last phase of his career, required tall tales of superhuman eating feats to go along with his legendary status.

Not all of Elvis's extravagances were bad for his health. He liked to collect ostentatious jewelry, fancy cars, and all kinds of guns; he was fascinated by law enforcement; and he was extremely generous. At the start of his career Elvis developed an image as an average, red-blooded, all-American male who would never wear any jewelry except a watch. Photographs of Elvis in the early days never show him wearing gaudy jewelry, but it's known that he had a fondness for diamond rings. In 1956 he donated an expensive custom-made diamond ring as a door prize for a charity event in Memphis. During the 1970s Elvis began to wear rings on all his fingers both onstage and off. He also wore heavy medallions, gold-plated belts, and chain-link bracelets. On a gold chain around his neck, Elvis wore a gold Star of David as well as a crucifix. He also liked to carry walking sticks adorned with tops made of silver or gold. Elvis also bought expensive jewelry for the Memphis Mafia, their wives, and his show business friends. He once gave Sammy Davis Jr. a $30,000 ring.

Elvis shows off one of his many automobiles to the fans.

The famous pink Cadillac that Elvis purchased for his mother has been variously identified as a 1955, a 1956, or a 1957 model. Most likely it was a slightly customized 1955 model.

Elvis had a lifelong love affair with Cadillacs. During his career he bought more than 100 Caddies for himself and the members of his entourage. One of the first cars Elvis purchased was a 1955 pink Cadillac sedan. He promptly gave the car to his mother, Gladys, despite the fact that she couldn't drive. This was the only Cadillac Elvis kept throughout his life, and it's still parked at Graceland. Elvis also bought unique foreign cars, such as a three-door Messerschmidt, as well as more prestigious automobiles, including a Mercedes limousine and a Rolls Royce. Elvis's most outrageous vehicle was his 1960 Cadillac limousine that had been customized by George Barris. It had 24-carat gold-dust paint and featured a motorized shoe-shine kit, a wet bar, a television, and a record player. The car was too cumbersome and impractical to use every day, and Elvis eventually loaned the gold Cadillac to MGM to promote one of his movies. The car, which is worth more than $100,000, is now on display in the Country Music Hall of Fame in Nashville.

Despite being able to buy any automobile he wanted, Elvis sometimes preferred this more traditional mode of transportation.

Elvis traveled with an entourage of buddies and bodyguards throughout most of his life, but the number of protectors increased after a series of death threats in the early 1970s.

Elvis also collected guns and other kinds of weapons. He was especially fond of a huge .44 magnum, a little Derringer similar to those carried by nineteenth-century riverboat gamblers, a turquoise-handled Colt .45, and a pearl-handled undercover .38. Elvis also lavished expensive guns on the members of the Memphis Mafia. His bodyguards, particularly Red and Sonny West, often carried weapons and so did Elvis. He once even boarded a commercial flight while packing a pistol. When the ticket agent followed him onto the plane to tell him he couldn't take a gun on board, Elvis left the plane in a huff. But the pilot came scurrying after him, apologized for the ticket agent, and allowed Elvis to get back on the airplane.

During the 1970s Elvis carried a gun at all times because he was concerned for his safety. After he began performing again in Las Vegas, Elvis received many death and kidnapping threats. He believed that assassins who tried to kill a famous person were seeking glory and media attention and would risk death or life in prision to get it. In 1971, while Elvis was performing in Las Vegas, an anonymous caller got through to his hotel room and warned him that there would be an assassination attempt during that evening's performance. Later that day Elvis received an International Hotel menu: His picture on the front had been defaced, and a handgun had been drawn near his heart. A message included with the menu read, "Guess who, and where?" The FBI was called in, which must have both thrilled and frightened Elvis, and the hotel management told him he did not have to go on. But Elvis stuck a Derringer in his boot and a .45 in his belt and did the show anyway.

During another incident in Las Vegas in 1973, four drunks suddenly bolted onstage during Elvis's midnight show. Red West subdued one of the men, while three members of the Memphis Mafia, Vernon Presley, and one of the Colonel's assistants scuffled with two others and eventually dragged them offstage. Elvis knocked the fourth man off the stage and sent him hurtling into the crowd. Then Elvis apologized to the audience, telling them he was sorry; that is, he was sorry he didn't break the man's neck. This statement brought down the house, and there was a seven-minute standing ovation from the crowd.

Over the next few years there were so many death threats and other incidents that bodyguards Red and Sonny West became cautious about allowing strangers to get near Elvis. Their tactics were often rough, and they were frequently criticized by other entertainers and industry officials. At least three lawsuits were filed against Elvis because of the strong-arm tactics of his guards. Elvis himself is said to have saved his violent aggression for television sets: He had a reputation for shooting the TV when something came on that he didn't want to see. The number of times Elvis actually shot out a television has probably been exaggerated, but he was known to have blasted several TVs with the Derringer he kept in his boot, particularly when singer Robert Goulet appeared on the screen.

Elvis's authentic narcotics agent's badge was given to him by President Richard Nixon.

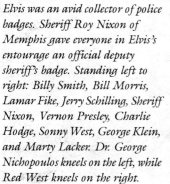

Elvis was an avid collector of police badges. Sheriff Roy Nixon of Memphis gave everyone in Elvis's entourage an official deputy sheriff's badge. Standing left to right: Billy Smith, Bill Morris, Lamar Fike, Jerry Schilling, Sheriff Nixon, Vernon Presley, Charlie Hodge, Sonny West, George Klein, and Marty Lacker. Dr. George Nichopoulos kneels on the left, while Red West kneels on the right.

Elvis was infatuated with law enforcement and collected police badges wherever he went. Elvis once asked the sheriff of Shelby County, Tennessee, for deputy's badges for himself, his father, his doctor, and most members of the Memphis Mafia. Elvis also had a badge from the Palm Springs Police Department, and he was close friends with members of the Los Angeles Police Department and the Denver Police. Considering that Elvis once had a reputation as a rebel who opposed authority, and was actually arrested in 1956 for fighting with two gas station attendants, it's ironic that he came to have so much respect and admiration for law enforcement.

Elvis was arrested in 1956 for fighting with a pair of belligerent gas station attendants in Memphis. Crowds cheered when Elvis was cleared of all charges.

In December 1970 Elvis made a spontaneous decision to go to Washington, D.C., to visit Deputy U.S. Narcotics Director John Finlator. Although Elvis said he was going to Washington to volunteer his help in the antidrug campaign, he was really hoping to obtain a federal narcotics badge and a complete set of credentials to add to his collection. Director Finlator turned down Elvis's request for a badge, but this didn't stop Elvis. He immediately decided to go over Finlator's head, and along with a couple of members of the Memphis Mafia, he went to call on President Nixon at the White House. It took Elvis only a few minutes of laying on the charm to talk Nixon into giving him an authentic narcotics agent's badge. By then, Elvis was on a roll, and he also convinced the president to give him souvenirs inscribed with the presidential seal for his bodyguards and their wives. On later trips to Washington, Elvis visited FBI headquarters to offer his assistance in fighting the war on drugs. While it's not surprising that Elvis was able to visit law enforcement agencies, the fact that he could get in to see the president on a few hours notice is an extraordinary testimony to Elvis's amazing popularity and power. Other entertainers are honored to be invited to perform at the White House, but Elvis simply dropped in to get something he wanted.

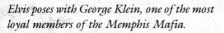

Elvis poses with George Klein, one of the most loyal members of the Memphis Mafia.

Despite his excessive lifestyle, Elvis was deeply interested in religion and spirituality. His behavior may not have always matched his beliefs, but Elvis always said that he believed that his talent and success came from God. He felt strongly that if he didn't extend some of his good fortune to other people, it could all be taken away from him. Throughout his career, Elvis recorded gospel albums that featured his favorite hymns. During the 1960s, actress Donna Douglas and several other friends encouraged Elvis to expand his beliefs by reading about religion. Later, Elvis's long-time hairdresser, Larry Geller, inspired him to read books on the occult, esoteric healing, and Eastern religions. Elvis became deeply involved with his reading and spent many evenings attempting to discuss what he had read with his buddies, who had a difficult time keeping up with Elvis's lofty pursuits. No matter what interested him, Elvis pursued it to the fullest, and during the time he was reading esoteric religious books, he became so immersed in his studies that his personality began to change. Rumor had it that at one point, Elvis decided he had special spiritual powers that allowed him to heal the sick and commune with nature. Everyone around him became concerned, and Colonel Parker decided he had to have a talk with Elvis about what he was doing. The Colonel persuaded Elvis that Geller was an unhealthy influence, and Elvis obligingly dropped Geller from his group of friends and toned down his interest in the occult.

Only Elvis could simply drop by to see the President of the United States. In December 1970, Elvis visited President Richard Nixon in the hopes of obtaining a special narcotics agent's badge to add to his collection.

Elvis introduced President Nixon to his friends Sonny West and Jerry Schilling.

Elvis bought a car for stranger Mennie Person simply because she had admired his limousine. Mrs. Person's daughter, Bassanta, is shown leaning against Elvis's gift.

The King may have had his faults and eccentricities, but he was regally generous. Elvis not only gave freely to his friends and their families, but he also frequently donated large amounts of money to charity and organized benefit concerts. Elvis was also kind to complete strangers, and he was said to have given cars to many people he didn't even know. Once while he was buying a couple of El Dorados for members of his entourage, Elvis noticed a young couple wandering around the dealer's lot trying to find a car they could afford. Elvis told them to pick any car they wanted, wrote out a check, and then left the salesman to do the paperwork. Another time he gave away seven Cadillacs and Lincolns to some people in Colorado. This inspired a local newscaster to joke on the air that he wouldn't mind having a little sports car. The next day a Cadillac Seville was delivered to the newsman. A Seville is hardly a sports car, but the man wasn't going to complain.

Elvis generously signs autographs at a gala event.

Elvis received dozens of awards during his lifetime. While some marked career achievements, others attested to his generous nature as a human being. On February 25, 1961, Elvis was honored with an "Elvis Presley Day," proclaimed by Tennessee governor Buford Ellington. Among the events celebrating the occasion were a luncheon at the Claridge Hotel and then two concerts by Elvis that evening. The proceeds went to support 38 charities, including the Elvis Presley Youth Center in Tupelo, Mississippi.

Elvis and the Colonel's Christmas cards to their business associates were variations on the same theme each year. The Colonel dressed as Santa Claus and Elvis dressed simply as Elvis. This one dates from the early 1960s.

By the mid-1970s, the Christmas cards were composite photos featuring images related to the Colonel's and Elvis's lives. Here the Colonel's St. Bernards get into the act. Notice both the traditional Christmas tree and the California palms.

Another of the Colonel's famous composite photos.

Elvis was also generous in less flamboyant ways. On the flight to Washington to see the president, Elvis noticed a soldier who was returning home for the Christmas holidays. Knowing firsthand how little money servicemen are paid, Elvis told his traveling companions to give the soldier all of their cash. They gave him about $500, which meant that Elvis and his friends had to rely on credit cards to pay for the rest of the trip. Another time Elvis gave $500 to a blind man who was selling pencils. When he read in the paper about a poverty-stricken black woman in dire need of a wheelchair, Elvis bought her a motorized chair and delivered it himself. Many times when he saw a news report about a police officer being killed, Elvis would call the television station to get the name of the officer's widow so he could send her money. At Christmas, Elvis and Vernon would donate $1,000 checks to over a hundred Memphis charities. Few entertainers could match Elvis's generosity.

Looking back at the last years of Elvis's life, with all the rumors about his habits and whims, there is no way that anyone but a superman could have done all the things, both good and bad, that Elvis is said to have done. Normal standards don't seem adequate to measure Elvis's life and achievements. The temptation to exaggerate is especially irresistible because Elvis truly was larger than life. Secluded behind the gates of Graceland, there wasn't anyone who had the power or authority to stop the King from indulging in whatever he chose. But for all of his desperate, self-destructive behavior, the one thing that remained primary was Elvis's incredible voice. It rang true and clear from the day he recorded "That's All Right" until June 26, 1977, the day he gave his final performance in Indianapolis's Market Square Arena.

CHAPTER FIFTEEN

THE KING IS DEAD

He was a rocker. I was a rocker.

I'm not rockin' anymore and

he's not rockin' anymore.

LITTLE RICHARD

Girlfriend Ginger Alden was the first to find Elvis's body, though initial reports claimed he had been found by road manager Joe Esposito.

Elvis Presley died at Graceland on August 16, 1977. He was 42 years old. Ginger Alden, a girlfriend, found him slumped over in the bathroom. Paramedics were called, but they failed to revive Elvis, and he was taken to Baptist Memorial Hospital where further attempts to resuscitate him failed. He was pronounced dead by his physician, Dr. George Nichopoulos, who listed the official cause of death as cardiac arrhythmia, or erratic heartbeat.

Almost immediately, rumors that Elvis was dead began to sift into Memphis newspaper offices and radio and television newsrooms, but reporters adopted a wait-and-see attitude. Many of them had heard rumors like this before, since crank calls often came into the newsroom. Sometimes the caller would say Elvis had been killed in a car accident or a plane crash, or that he'd been shot by the jealous boyfriend of a woman he was dating. Once it was even reported that Elvis had drowned in a submarine. The King was a hometown boy, and he was a constant source of news, some of which was manufactured for or by the Memphis press. Newspaper editors and newsroom managers were cautious about sending out reporters if the rumor that Elvis was dead was just another hoax. But when the staff of the *Memphis Press-Scimitar* learned from a trusted source that Elvis was actually dead, the newsroom became unusually silent. Dan Sears of radio station WMPS in Memphis made the first official announcement, and WHBQ-TV was the first television station to interrupt its programming with the terrible news.

As reports of Elvis's death spread across the country, radio stations immediately began to play his records. Some stations quickly organized tributes to Elvis while others simply played his music at the request of listeners, many of whom were in a state of shock. Some people called their favorite radio stations because they wanted to tell someone about the first time they heard Elvis sing or to talk about how much Elvis and his music had meant to them. Just as many people remember exactly where they were when they heard that President John F. Kennedy had been killed, most of Elvis's fans remember where they were the day Elvis died. Mick Fleetwood of the rock group Fleetwood Mac recalls, "The news came over like a ton of bricks. I was driving back from the mountains and I had the radio on. They were playing an Elvis medley and I thought, 'Great.' And then they came back with the news."

The way the major television networks handled Elvis's death demonstrates his enormous popularity and the tremendous impact he had on America. Few people realized the true scope of that impact before his death, but it quickly became apparent the day he died. Data from the television ratings service Arbitron reveal that on the day Elvis died there was a huge increase in the number of televisions tuned to evening news programs. Elvis's death was a late-breaking story, and there was not enough time for TV reporters who had been sent to Memphis to file stories for the evening news. Executives had to decide quickly what film footage they could use from their files and where to place the story in relation to the other news of the day.

The staff of NBC-TV not only rewrote their news lineup to lead off with the story of Elvis's death, but they also made immediate plans to delay *The Tonight Show* and put together a late-night news documentary. David Brinkley was a national news anchor for NBC at that time, and he opened his broadcast with three minutes devoted to Elvis's sudden death. ABC-TV also decided to lead off with the Presley story. When they learned that NBC would be doing a late-night news special about Elvis's contribution to American music, ABC announced that they would also air a half-hour documentary.

The CBS Evening News with Walter Cronkite had led the ratings for news programs for more than a decade. Cronkite was the most respected person in broadcasting at that time, and the CBS executives were so sure of their number-one position that they decided not to handle Elvis's death the same way as the other two networks. CBS didn't open their evening news broadcast with a story about Elvis. The Arbitron records show that when viewers realized this, millions of them immediately switched to another channel. The CBS decision not to lead with Elvis's death gave the CBS Evening News its lowest ratings in years. (For the record, Roger Mudd was substituting for Walter Cronkite that evening.) CBS devoted only 70 seconds to a story on Elvis, which ran after a lengthy segment on the Panama Canal. The producer for that evening's news was vehemently opposed to leading off with Elvis's death, even though other CBS executives suggested it repeatedly. Interviewed later, the producer admitted that he was out of sync with the national consciousness. Two days later, CBS tried to save face by putting together a documentary on Elvis.

A mourner outside the gates of Graceland is overcome with grief.

Within an hour of the reports of Elvis's death, mourners began gathering in front of Graceland.

Fan club members, fiercely loyal to Elvis to the end, were among the mourners who held vigil at the Music Gate.

Within an hour after Elvis's death, fans began to gather in front of Graceland. By the next day, when the gates were opened for mourners to view Elvis's body, the crowd was estimated at about 20,000. By the time the gates closed at 6:30, about 80,000 fans had passed by Elvis's coffin. People came from all parts of the country and from all over the world. Eventually so many mourners arrived that it was impossible for all of them to be admitted to Graceland, even with extended calling hours. Law enforcement officials were afraid there would be problems with crowd control, but only one unfortunate incident occurred, when a drunk driver careened into a group of teenagers, killing two of them.

Like every event in Elvis's career, press coverage of his death was so heavy that reporters and photographers generated publicity about the publicity.

Medics and ambulances were stationed nearby to treat those who were stricken by the heat.

As the number of mourners around the gates of Graceland grew, a carnival atmosphere developed; people hawking T-shirts and other souvenirs began to work the crowd. The people who were unable to get into Graceland to pay their last respects to Elvis consoled one another by exchanging anecdotes about their idol. When reporters asked why they were there, people inevitably gave the same reply: They didn't really know, but they wanted to be where Elvis was this one last time. The hot Memphis weather and close crush of the crowd caused many people to faint. A medic was stationed near the entrance to Graceland, but no one left because of the heat.

The intense summer heat was made more unbearable by the crushing crowds in front of Graceland. Many mourners were overcome by the heat and by exhaustion, yet no one left.

Out-of-town fans and local residents line the streets of Memphis to catch a glimpse of the funeral procession.

Arrangements in the shape of guitars, hound dogs, stars, lightning bolts, and crowns were sent by mourners and fan clubs.

Some floral arrangements reflected aspects of Elvis's life that only fans could decipher. Thousands of flowers sent by fans from around the country are combined into one massive display at Forest Hill Cemetery, where Elvis was originally buried.

Elvis's fans sent a tremendous array of flowers, which were set out along the bank in front of the house. Every blossom in Memphis had been sold by the afternoon of August 17, and additional flowers were shipped in from other parts of the country. It was the biggest day in the history of FTD (a florists' delivery service). The company claims that more than 2,150 arrangements were delivered. Fans sent arrangements shaped like lightning bolts, guitars, hound dogs, and stars, as well as more traditional wreaths and bouquets. Many of the flowers were sent immediately to Forest Hill Cemetery, where Elvis was to be buried. After the funeral, Vernon chose to carry on the tradition of always thinking of the fans; he allowed them to take away all the flowers as souvenirs.

Many celebrities attended Elvis's funeral, including Caroline Kennedy, country music guitarist Chet Atkins, performers Ann-Margret and George Hamilton, and television evangelist Rex Humbard, who was one of the speakers during the service. Comedian Jackie Kahane, who had opened many of Elvis's concert performances, delivered the eulogy, and a local minister also spoke. The singers for the service were gospel performers Jake Hess, J.D. Sumner, James Blackwood, and their vocal groups, and Kathy Westmoreland. The casket was carried to Forest Hill Cemetery in a long cortege of white automobiles. Later, after someone threatened to steal Elvis's remains, his casket was moved to Meditation Gardens behind Graceland, where other members of the Presley family—Gladys, Vernon, and Minnie Mae—are also now buried. Gladys's body was moved to Meditation Gardens in 1977; Vernon Presley died in 1979; and Minnie Mae Presley died in 1980.

Those who attended the private funeral service included family members, old friends, and business associates from throughout Elvis's career. Reverend C.W. Bradley officiated.

The casket is carried into the chapel at the cemetery. There were five official pallbearers, including Elvis's road manager Joe Eposito, his doctor George Nichopoulos, cousin Billy Smith, bandmember Charlie Hodge, and friend Lamar Fike.

Ann-Margret and husband Roger Smith were among the celebrities who attended the funeral.

Actor George Hamilton (center) also attended. Colonel Parker, dressed in blue, can be seen standing next to him.

The funeral procession enters the grounds of Forest Hill Cemetery.

A white hearse carried Elvis's body.

The official funeral procession consisted of sixteen white automobiles; unofficially, dozens of other vehicles followed.

On August 1, 1977, just 15 days before Elvis died, Ballantine Books had published a book put together by Steve Donleavy called *Elvis: What Happened?* It consisted of interviews with three of Elvis's former bodyguards—Red West, Sonny West, and Dave Hebler. The three men were the first to come forward with stories of Elvis's unusual lifestyle. *Elvis: What Happened?* included accounts of his mood swings, his relationships with women, and his excessive use of prescription drugs. The book received almost no publicity until Bob Greene, a columnist for the *Chicago Sun-Times,* interviewed Sonny West for his syndicated column. The article happened to run on the day that Elvis died. Greene's column provoked a great deal of protest from fans across the country as well as from several journalists, including Geraldo Rivera, who blasted Donleavy on *Good Morning America* for smearing Elvis's name.

The bodyguards' story was difficult to believe. Nothing like it had surfaced before because, for the most part, Elvis had been able to keep his eccentric habits and erratic behavior out of the press. Donleavy also lacked credibility. He had been a reporter for the *National Enquirer* when he started working on the book, and he was employed by the controversial *New York Post* when it was published. Donleavy also appeared on the NBC documentary about Elvis that aired on the evening he died. Donleavy made the mistake of using the term "white trash" in reference to Elvis, and this didn't go over very well with his fans. So Donleavy was popular with neither the public nor the press. Because Vernon had fired the three bodyguards the previous year, many people believed that their outrageous account of Elvis's life was just sour grapes, and that Donleavy had manipulated the story to be as sensational as possible.

Over the next two years, reports of Elvis's drug abuse and its possible connection with his death surfaced occasionally, but few people paid much attention to them. Ironically, it was Geraldo Rivera who helped uncover the truth about Elvis's drug abuse. In 1979, Rivera and Charles Thompson, a producer for the television news magazine *20/20,* obtained a copy of a confidential report by Bioscience Laboratory, which had analyzed specimens taken during the postmortem on Elvis. The report indicated that Elvis's death was the result of polypharmacy, or the interaction of several drugs taken at the same time. A few days later the *New York Times* ran a story that backed Rivera's findings.

Dave Hebler was one of the bodyguards involved with the controversial biography, Elvis: What Happened?

Sonny West, another author of the so-called bodyguard book, had worked for Elvis for almost two decades.

Elvis's physician, Dr. George Nichopoulos, was acquitted of charges of overprescribing drugs to Elvis and singer Jerry Lee Lewis.

In 1980 Elvis's physician, Dr. George Nichopoulos, had his medical license suspended for three months and was placed on three years probation. In 1981 Nichopolous was charged with 14 counts of "willingly and feloniously" overprescribing drugs for Elvis. He was acquitted, but many people came to view him as a villain. During a football game in Memphis in 1979, someone took a shot at Nichopolous but missed.

The spontaneous outpouring of grief over Elvis's death, the extended coverage by the news media, and the offering of condolences from around the world were very much like the mourning that occurs when a president dies. As hundreds of editorials attempted to summarize Elvis's place in our culture, the whole nation seemed to realize that Elvis had changed the way we look, the music we listen to, the way we talk, and the kind of hero we believe in. At the time, many people felt that Elvis's death marked the end of an era as well as the end of a legendary career, but this has not proved to be the case. Even though Elvis is dead, his legend continues to grow with each new revelation about his personal life and each reinterpretation of his contribution to our culture.

A poignant image: Vernon Presley, filled with a sorrow no words can describe, places a rose on his son's grave.

"There's no way to measure his impact on society or the void that he leaves. He will always be the King of Rock 'n' Roll"—Pat Boone, 1977

229

CHAPTER SIXTEEN

LONG LIVE THE

KING

A whole industry was built

around an animated mouse named Mickey.

The next could be Elvis Presley.

JOSEPH RASCOFF

BUSINESS MANAGER OF THE PRESLEY ESTATE

1982

 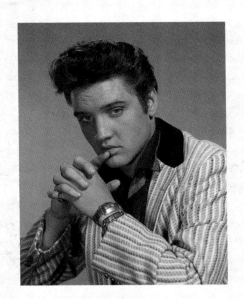 

 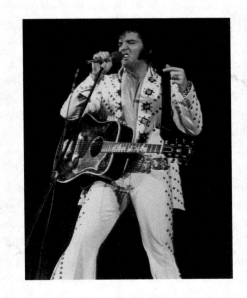 

Elvis had an extraordinary 23-year career in show business. He was an artistic and financial success, and he made an enormous impact on popular music. But since his death, Elvis has become a phenomenon. Elvis's popularity has not diminished, and each new piece of information about his life that comes to light serves to keep his name in the news. Since Elvis died there has been an increase in the merchandising of his music and an explosion of Elvis Presley products.

Elvis's continued popularity is owed to the loyalty of his fans, who have more or less created their own legendary Elvis since the death of the King. When Elvis died, he left a void in the lives of his fans, and they've attempted to fill it with conventions, rituals, fan clubs, and other activities. Their intense devotion dates back to the beginning of Elvis's career as a country singer. Country music fans tend to be more loyal than fans of other kinds of music. Many people who love country music remain devoted to a particular performer for decades, and they often inspire their children to become fans as well. Many of Elvis's most devoted fans first became interested in him when he was a country singer, and they remained loyal to him even though his music evolved and changed.

Elvis always tried to give his fans what they wanted. In the 1950s his audience came to see his notorious performing style, hoping he would go further at each appearance than he'd gone before. Elvis was able to whip his audiences into a frenzy that people who aren't fans simply can't understand. In the 1960s his fans paid to see Elvis's musical films, even though some of his vehicles were badly produced. Although Elvis had wanted to be a serious actor when he went to Hollywood, his attempts at dramatic roles were not successful at the box office. Colonel Parker was able to persuade Elvis to continue making musical comedies by telling him that this was the kind of movie his fans wanted to see. In the 1970s audiences expected Elvis to perform certain songs, wear his trademark jumpsuits, and strike specific poses. Elvis obligingly followed a pattern that catered to his fans from about 1970 until he died.

In the 1950s and 1970s, when Elvis was onstage, there was always a lot of interaction between Elvis and his audience. Elvis liked to single out certain women in the audience and perform specifically for them, breaking down the usual barrier between performer and spectator. Throwing towels into the audience and tossing his capes or personal jewelry into the crowd also brought him close to the audience, and his fans responded in kind by throwing underwear, keys, flowers, and stuffed animals onto the stage. Elvis's fans went to concerts not only to see him perform but also to be in contact with their idol. Even the fans who did not have an opportunity to touch him or relate with him one to one could do so vicariously through those who were able to get close to Elvis.

Elvis's uncle, Vester Presley, was the head guard at the gates of Graceland for many years.

Following Elvis's burial, Vernon allowed the fans to take home the thousands of funeral flowers as mementos of the occasion.

From the early days of his fame until the end of his life, when Vernon let the fans take Elvis's funeral flowers, the people involved in Elvis's career always treated his fans well. Elvis believed that his success depended on his fans, and he was always grateful for their loyalty and love. When he was young, he had allowed them access to his personal life that no other entertainer would dare. Before Elvis moved to Graceland, when fans would hang around the Presleys' home, Elvis would often invite them onto the patio, and Gladys occasionally served them iced tea. At Graceland fans often gathered at the gate, and Elvis would walk or ride one of his horses down to sign autographs. Elvis's Uncle Vester, who was one of the guards at the gatehouse, often stood and talked with fans for hours.

A statue commemorating Elvis was sculpted by Eric Parks and erected in Memphis in 1980.

No matter how difficult the fans may have made Elvis's life by forcing him to live in seclusion, he never complained publicly; he always had nice things to say to the press about his fans. Colonel Tom Parker gave premiums to Elvis's fan clubs and donated Elvis's personal belongings to be auctioned off for charity. Elvis once presented a car to the president of one of his fan clubs. When he was on tour during the 1950s, Elvis gave as many interviews to reporters for high-school newspapers and fan-club newsletters as he did to reporters from big-city papers.

Despite the fact that Elvis became a very wealthy man, he never forgot that he was a Southern boy with humble beginnings. He didn't move to Hollywood, but kept his home in Memphis, where he greatly benefited local businesses and contributed generously to many charitable organizations. Elvis never completely lost his Southern accent, and he always preferred down-home cooking and the company of other good ol' boys. Elvis let his fans know in many ways that he had always been one of them. Despite his money, position, and power, he never acted as though he were better than his fans. Elvis was one of the people and proud of it, and they were proud of him.

The almost continuous release of controversial biographical information about Elvis keeps his name in the news. Immediately following his death, and perhaps in response to *Elvis: What Happened?*, biographies by other former employees began to appear. Some of these books vehemently denied that Elvis abused drugs or showed signs of erratic behavior. Even though most of these biographies claimed to be inside stories, the books that emphasize Elvis's good behavior were written by employees who actually had little day-to-day contact with him. *My Life with Elvis* by Becky Yancey and Cliff Linedecker claims to be the "fond memories of a fan who became Elvis's private secretary." The book relates several lighthearted anecdotes about Elvis, including how Yancey met him: She threw up on him after riding a roller coaster. May Mann, a former Hollywood gossip columnist, extolled Elvis's virtues in her book, *Elvis, Why Won't They Leave You Alone?* She claimed that she wrote her book because Elvis asked her to; he wanted Lisa Marie to know the truth.

Members of the Memphis Mafia also published books about Elvis. Jerry Hopkins wrote *Elvis: The Final Years*, and Marty and Patsy Lacker collaborated on *Elvis: Portrait of a Friend*. Both of these books confirm the stories in *Elvis: What Happened?* about Elvis's drug use and destructive lifestyle. It was as though a battle line had been drawn between the people who had known Elvis personally: On one side were people who insisted there was only a "good Elvis"; on the other side were people who maintained that he also had bad habits and characteristics.

By the 1980s, professional writers and scholars had begun to publish books about Elvis. Albert Goldman's controversial biography, *Elvis*, is probably the most notorious account of Elvis's life. In addition to his drug problems, Goldman's biography speculates that Elvis had an unhealthy attachment to his mother as well as to his friends in the Memphis Mafia. He also describes in detail certain aspects of Elvis's bizarre lifestyle, including his eating habits and his dangerous games with firearms. Rock-music historian Dave Marsh's eloquent book, *Elvis*, concentrates on the singer's contributions to popular music and culture.

The statue of Elvis is located in Memphis's Elvis Presley Plaza, which is just south of the downtown area.

Later biographies by members of Elvis's family acknowledge his bad side but balance these stories with anecdotes about his generosity. *The Touch of Two Kings* by Elvis's stepbrother Rick Stanley (who is now a minister) recounts Stanley's experiences with his famous relative. *Elvis, We Loved You Tender* by his stepmother, Dee Stanley, is a compassionate look at Elvis's ups and downs during the 1960s and 1970s. Priscilla Beaulieu Presley's account of her relationship with Elvis in *Elvis and Me* provides much-needed insight into Elvis's secluded life during the 1960s.

Elaine Dundy's *Elvis and Gladys* is as much a biography of Gladys Love Smith Presley as it is of Elvis. The book traces Gladys's genealogy back to her great-great-great-grandmother, Morning White Dove. Dundy follows Elvis's life up until 1958, the year Gladys died, and this warm-hearted biography is an excellent account of Elvis's early years in Tupelo. It doesn't dwell on the negative side of the singer because of its limited scope.

In 1987 Lucy de Barbin published a controversial account of her love affair with Elvis entitled *Are You Lonesome Tonight?* De Barbin claimed that in 1956 Elvis fathered one of her daughters. Her dubious story was quickly overshadowed by rumors that Elvis was still alive. The credibility of these reports was promoted by a self-published book by Gail B. Giorgio entitled *The Most Incredible Elvis Presley Story Ever Told* and by a song by Texas record producer Major Bill Smith called "Hey! Big E." The rumors led to reported sightings of Elvis in fast-food restaurants in Michigan. In 1988 Giorgio's book was republished as *Is Elvis Alive?* to take advantage of the current surge of interest in

Elvis. As proof of her incredible claim that Elvis is alive, Giorgio includes an audiocassette of Elvis's voice with each book. On the cassette you hear what is supposed to be Elvis's voice discussing events that have occurred since his death.

On June 7, 1982, Graceland was opened to the public for the first time. Graceland was not just Elvis's home; it was his retreat from the pressures of making movies, recording music, and touring in concert. Having endured the death of his mother, his divorce from Priscilla, and two major career changes, Elvis felt that Graceland was the only constant in his life. It was the center of his world, and it remained intact when the rest of his life seemed to be falling apart. When Graceland was opened to the public, Elvis's fans could actually see where the important events of his life had taken place and relive his legend as they walked over the grounds. Many rooms on the main floor and in the basement are open to the public, but the kitchen area and all of the bedrooms, including the bedroom that Elvis used, are kept strictly private.

Elvis purchased Graceland, located on the outskirts of Memphis, in March 1957. A month later, he showed off his new, luxurious home to Hollywood starlet Yvonne Lime.

Elvis bought Graceland in March 1957. He and his parents had decided they should move from their ranch-style house on Audubon Drive in Memphis because it gave them no privacy from Elvis's fans. At the time Elvis purchased Graceland, the area around the house was still mostly rolling countryside. Graceland was in the township of Whitehaven, which had not yet been incorporated into Memphis. Elvis purchased the 18-room home, which sits on top of a small hill, and 14 acres of land for about $100,000. Virginia Grant, the real estate agent who sold the property, has written a short memoir entitled *Exactly as It Happened: How Elvis Bought Graceland* in which she recounts the details of the sale. At first, Grant had looked for another ranch-style house for the Presleys, but when Gladys told her that Elvis wanted a large Colonial home, Grant realized she had been on the wrong track: "Without hesitation, and as if God himself put the thought in my mind and the words on my tongue, I immediately picked Graceland as the home for them, though I had never been in the house myself."

Located at what is now 3764 Elvis Presley Boulevard, Graceland was built in 1939 by Dr. Thomas Moore and his wife, Ruth, at a time when the road that now rushes past it was known as U.S. Highway 51. The estate was named in honor of Ruth Moore's aunt, Grace Toof. The house is faced with pink Tennessee fieldstone and has a white-columned portico reminiscent of plantation houses in the antebellum South. The house

When Elvis first lived at Graceland, the surrounding area was mostly rolling countryside.

Elvis's home was first opened to the public in 1982, an event much heralded by his fans.

The white-columned portico of the main house is in the style of the much-beloved architecture of the antebellum South.

Graceland is almost as recognizable as Elvis himself, and many souvenir photographs depict Elvis and his home in odd ways. Here the famous statue of Elvis is shown in the front yard of Graceland, though the two icons are located miles apart.

Elvis enjoyed illuminating the grounds of Graceland with colored lights, particularly during the Christmas season.

Graceland is located at 3764 Elvis Presley Boulevard, formerly U.S. Highway 51.

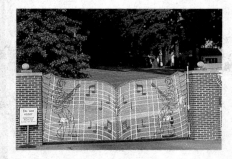

The famous Music Gate in front of Graceland was constructed by a local Memphis company.

Elvis and the Memphis Mafia often greeted fans at the Music Gate, particularly during the 1960s. Elvis's willingness to talk with fans on a one-to-one basis was part of the reason they held a vigil outside of Graceland whenever he was in town.

is too small to be called a mansion, but it is grand in manner, if not in scale. In the six months after he bought the house, Elvis spent about $500,000 remodeling Graceland to suit his tastes and his family's needs. Eventually the house was expanded to 23 rooms, including eight bathrooms. This was just about enough space for all the friends and family members Elvis liked to have around him.

In addition to the remodeling, an eight-foot-high pink fieldstone fence was built around the property to help control the crowds of fans who had become accustomed to dropping by. The famous Music Gate is set into the fence at the bottom of the driveway facing the main road. Designed by John Dillars, Sr., the wrought-iron gate features two guitar-wielding figures against a background of musical notes. Supposedly the notes represent the opening bar of "Love Me Tender."

Until Elvis was inducted into the army, Vernon and Gladys lived in the main house at Graceland. After his mother's death, when the rest of the family returned from Germany where Elvis was stationed, Vernon and his new wife, Dee, lived in another house nearby. A downstairs bedroom in Graceland was used by Elvis's grandmother, Minnie Mae Presley, until she died in 1980. It's now occupied by Elvis's Aunt Delta Mae Biggs, who at one time kept house at Graceland. Over the years many other relatives and friends lived either in Graceland or on the grounds. According to the terms of his will, Elvis's only child, Lisa Marie, was to have inherited Graceland on her twenty-fifth birthday, but she has decided to relinquish control of the estate until she turns 30 in 1998.

There are no antiques at Graceland; all of the furnishings are obviously new. The dire poverty of Elvis's childhood left him with a lifelong hatred of anything old. As he put it, "When I was growing up in Tupelo, I lived with enough . . . antiques to do me for a lifetime." But contrary to some reports, Graceland is not tasteless or tacky. The house is ostentatious, even flamboyant, but the interior design of the main floor is no different from the homes of many wealthy people in the 1950s.

Elvis, grandma Minnie Mae Presley, and Priscilla posed for a family photo in the mid-1960s. Elvis affectionately called his grandmother "Dodger."

A portrait of Priscilla Presley holding daughter Lisa Marie hangs in one of the first-floor rooms at Graceland.

The pool room at Graceland features an enormous stained-glass lamp.

The music room includes the piano that Priscilla had gilded for Elvis for their first wedding anniversary.

The jungle room has become the most talked-about part of Graceland, undoubtedly because of its eccentric decor.

The living room, dining room, and music room are on the main floor. These rooms are all decorated with gilt furniture, silky fabrics, elaborate drapes, crystal chandeliers, marble or mirror paneling, and wall-to-wall carpeting. The walls, carpeting, and most of the furniture are white. The curtains and some furnishings are blue, which was Elvis's favorite color. In 1974 Linda Thompson, Elvis's girlfriend at that time, had many of the furnishings changed to bright red, but when Graceland was opened to the public, Elvis's family returned them to their original color. The music room is predominantly gold and has a 1928 concert grand piano that Priscilla had gilded for Elvis on their first wedding anniversary.

The rooms designed for Elvis's personal use are more flamboyant than the other rooms in Graceland. These basement rooms reflect Elvis's personal style. The TV room has mirrors on the ceiling and a wrap-around, mirrored soda fountain, which at one time dispensed Pepsi, Gatorade, and spring water. The focal point of the room is a bank of three televisions that are set side by side in a wall unit. Elvis got the idea for this arrangement from President Lyndon Johnson, who liked to watch the news simultaneously on three networks. The TV room is predominantly blue and gold. On one wall there's a supergraphic of a TCB lightning bolt.

The pool room is across the hall from the TV room. It's decorated with hundreds of yards of patchwork-printed fabric on the walls and ceiling. A large stained-glass lamp hangs over the pool table, where Elvis enjoyed playing his favorite billiard game, eight ball. Interior designer Bill Eubanks helped decorate some of the rooms at Graceland, including the pool room, but Elvis was always very specific about how he wanted a room to look. Elvis selected most of the fabrics and furniture for Graceland himself although he occasionally got help from people whose opinions he trusted.

The jungle room was Elvis's favorite. The 40-foot-long room contains massive pieces of heavy furniture with fake-fur upholstery. The story goes that after Elvis saw a commercial for a Memphis furniture store called Donald's, he decided on the spur of the moment to drive down to the store and take a look at what was in stock. Within 30 minutes he'd picked out enough furniture for the entire jungle room, and everything was delivered that same day. The room has a Tahitian motif, with hand-carved thrones and varnished, scallop-edged Cypress tables accented with wooden lamps carved to resemble angry gods. To complement the tropical furniture, there is green shag carpeting on the floor and ceiling and a built-in waterfall with colored lights.

The main floor of Graceland is decorated in shades of blue and white.

The small, simple photograph of Vernon and Gladys below the imposing portrait of Elvis makes a poignant image.

The dining room is located on the main floor, though Elvis preferred to eat in the less formal atmosphere of the kitchen.

The TV room, painted in blue and gold, features a bank of three televisions, an idea pioneered by President Lyndon Johnson.

The 126 gold and platinum records that Elvis received during his career not only make an impressive display but are reminders of Elvis's tremendous achievements in the recording field.

If the main house represents Elvis the family man, then the trophy room, located behind Graceland proper, is a shrine to Elvis the legend.

Some of the bejeweled jumpsuits that Elvis wore in concert are also on view in the trophy room. Family members have always claimed that the stones and gems on these suits are real.

Costumes and attire representing specific moments in Elvis's life and career are on exhibit in the trophy room.

The trophy room at Graceland is a shrine to the legendary Elvis. Located in a separate building just south of the main house, it contains a vast collection of Elvis memorabilia. His seventh-grade achievement test is displayed alongside his 126 gold and platinum records and albums. Also on view are many of the jeweled jumpsuits Elvis wore in the 1970s, the black brocade tuxedo and white wedding dress in which Elvis and Priscilla were married, and some of his favorite jewelry. A wall display of Elvis's firearms and police badges hangs near a glass case that holds two of the three Grammy Awards he won for his inspirational recordings. (Ironically, Elvis never won a Grammy for his rock music.) Elvis's fans are represented in the trophy room by displays of letters requesting that he not be drafted, eccentric gifts that they showered onto Elvis, and telegrams sent from around the world offering condolences when he died.

Elvis also owned 11 acres of land across the highway from Graceland. At one time, he talked about building a movie theater. His private plane, the *Lisa Marie,* currently sits on the property. The *Lisa Marie* is a former Delta Airlines passenger plane that Elvis purchased in 1975. He had the plane customized to his specifications: the interior was fitted with a king-size bed, and the exterior was painted with the TCB logo, complete with lightning bolt.

The Lisa Marie, *currently located across the street from Graceland, was customized to suit Elvis's extravagant tastes.*

This small plaque in the cockpit of the Lisa Marie *symbolizes the humility of Elvis.*

Two years before his death, Elvis purchased a passenger jet which he quickly dubbed the Lisa Marie.

Customized floral arrangements are highlights of the annual commemoration of Elvis's death.

The emotional high-point of any visit to Graceland is Elvis's grave in Meditation Gardens behind the main house. A brick and white columned peristyle encloses the small space in which Elvis, his parents, and his grandmother are buried. An eternal flame burns at the head of Elvis's grave. There is no headstone; only a bronze plaque that bears a touching epitaph written by his father.

Some of the unique flower sculptures come in the shape of hound dogs, an important part of the Elvis legend.

A number of tributes are organized during the anniversary week to give the fans a special opportunity to remember Elvis.

Each year on the anniversary of Elvis's death, thousands of fans brave the sweltering August heat in Memphis to remember their idol. They have organized a week of tributes and memorials that includes visiting Graceland, Sun Records, and other Presley haunts. The week culminates in a candlelight ceremony. This ritual has been enacted every year since Elvis's death. On the evening of August 15, fans gather in front of the Music Gate. They sing some of Elvis's songs and swap Elvis stories. At 11:00 p.m., two or more Graceland employees walk down to the gate with a torch that has been lighted from the eternal flame. As the Music Gate swings open, the fans, each carrying a lighted candle, climb silently and reverently up the hill behind the house and walk single file past the grave site. The procession can take as long as four hours to pass through Meditation Gardens. It is not only a gesture of respect for Elvis, but it's also proof that Elvis's fans are as faithful after his death as they were during his lifetime. Their devotion reaches beyond the grave.

Thousands of people pour through Meditation Gardens each August 16th to pay their emotional respects to the King.

Elvis's grave has no headstone but is covered instead by a bronze plaque, which features a touching inscription written by his father, Vernon. An eternal flame burns at the head of the grave.

Elvis memorabilia is a thriving enterprise. Dolls such as this one are often worth hundreds of dollars.

Vernon Presley, looking tired and drained, leaves probate court after discussing Elvis's will. Vernon was named executor.

The fans aren't alone in remembering the anniversary of Elvis's death. Each year, promoters, collectors, and manufacturers who market and sell commemorative items and souvenirs mark the passing of another year. Significant dates, such as the tenth anniversary of Elvis's death or his fiftieth birthday, increase the amount of Elvis merchandise that goes on sale. The diversity of Elvis products is overwhelming and often amusing: from clothing, shampoo, and liquor decanters to lamps, board games, and dolls. Almost every imaginable product has been transformed into an Elvis souvenir, memento, or collectible. Even dirt from the grounds of Graceland and sweat supposedly from Elvis's body are available for purchase. The enormous variety of these collectibles and the crass commercialism behind some of them have attracted a lot of attention. Catalogs of Elvis merchandise are available, and newspaper and television features have spotlighted collectors of Elvis memorabilia.

The marketing of Elvis Presley is hardly a new phenomenon. As far back as 1956, Colonel Parker had begun negotiating with promoter Henry G. Saperstein for the rights to manufacture products with Elvis's picture on them. In the 1950s, Elvis's name and face showed up on lipstick, charm bracelets, jeans, and countless other items. After Elvis died, Parker continued to manage the star's business. Minutes after he heard about Elvis's death, Parker supposedly muttered, "Nothing has changed. This won't change anything." By the time Elvis was buried, Parker had made a deal with Factors, Inc., to market Elvis products. The Colonel got Vernon Presley's signature to seal the deal on the day of Elvis's funeral.

In 1980 the executors of Elvis's estate, including Priscilla Presley (Vernon had died in 1979), petitioned the court for approval of all financial transactions made with Parker on behalf of the estate for the purposes of establishing a trust fund. A court-appointed attorney, Blanchard E. Tual, investigated Parker's management of Elvis from the beginning of his career to his final deal with Factors, Inc. This inquiry resulted in a court case charging Parker with "enriching himself by mismanaging Presley's career." The judge ordered the Presley estate to stop all dealings with Parker and to sue him to recover at least part of the money the Colonel was responsible for losing. In 1983 the estate attempted to sue Parker, who sought dismissal of the lawsuit on the grounds that he was not an American citizen and could not be sued under federal law. For the first

Across the street from Graceland are souvenir shops that specialize in Elvis mementos and collectibles.

time, the Colonel admitted that he had been born in Holland and had never been a U.S. citizen. The case was settled out of court. In 1984 a court in Tennessee decided that the Presley estate controlled the rights to Elvis Presley's name and likeness, and that all royalties would go to the estate.

The marketing of Elvis souvenirs is a small business venture compared to the marketing of his music. Before his death in 1977, Elvis had sold 250 million records worldwide. Immediately after his death, record stores across the country quickly sold out of Elvis's records. RCA's pressing plants operated 24 hours a day to fill the new orders for Elvis's records that began to pour in. For a while the record company subcontracted other pressing companies to keep up with the demand. In September RCA still had not caught up with all of the orders. RCA's plants outside the U.S. found themselves in the same position and were operating day and night. One factory in Hamburg, West Germany, supposedly pressed nothing but Elvis's records in an attempt to meet the demand of fans in that country. By October, sales were still so high in the United States that several of Elvis's albums were on the charts once again.

The Elvis Presley Museum, also located across from Graceland, is owned and operated by Jimmy Velvet. The museum features jewelry, automobiles, and articles of clothing connected with Elvis's life and career.

Even though Elvis was dead, RCA continued to release his albums at the rate of two or three per year. Over time, the rate of release has declined. As was the case while he was alive, some of the albums were well-received while others were criticized for their inferior quality. The marketing strategy behind the albums varied as much as the quality. Some albums, such as *Guitar Man*, used advanced technology to update Elvis's sound. Other albums, such as *He Walks Beside Me—Favorite Songs of Faith and Inspiration*, contained previously released material repackaged yet another time. Some albums were the result of record producers at RCA searching the vaults for any unreleased recording of Elvis's voice. *Elvis—Greatest Hits Vol. 4*, for example, contained previously released cuts in addition to never-before-released live material from Las Vegas, Hawaii, and Nashville.

The unrelenting marketing of Elvis's image leaves some fans cold.

In 1983 a record producer from RCA found master tapes and records stored at Graceland, some of which contained unreleased live performances and offstage conversations with Elvis. In 1985 RCA released much of the musical material in a six-album set to celebrate Elvis's fiftieth birthday. Even though the company is often criticized for recycling material too often and for doling out new material in bits and pieces, RCA continues to be the sole distributor of Elvis's music.

Graffiti on the stone fence at Graceland is sometimes poignant, sometimes bitter, sometimes sexual—but always interesting.

The Elvis impersonators are a remarkable part of the Elvis legend. Often ridiculed by the press, most see their occupation as a mission to keep Elvis's image and name alive. Fans agree.

The Elvis impersonators are perhaps the most curious offshoot of the Elvis phenomenon; they are also the most ridiculed. Some Elvis impersonators were performing before Elvis died, but in recent years more and more actors have made a career out of imitating Elvis. Some even have plastic surgery to make their faces and bodies resemble his. Their acts consist entirely of imitating Elvis—his singing and performing style, his appearance, his mannerisms, and his speech patterns. Most impersonators limit themselves to imitating Elvis as he appeared in Las Vegas. Many of them keep up the ruse offstage as well. The fans never mistake the impersonators for the real Elvis nor do they expect them to be as talented and charismatic as Elvis, or even to look exactly like him. Elvis impersonators allow his fans to relive the excitement of his live performances.

Those who try to find the secret of Elvis's tremendous popularity will not find it among the tacky souvenirs and commemorative items. The key lies in the handwritten notes left by fans on his grave at Graceland—notes filled with sincere tributes that quickly disappear through the ravages of weather, like so many tears in the rain. Elvis's fans are the most eloquent testimony to his enormous talent and his lasting impact on all of us.

Keeping the faith, 1957.

The fans speak via the stone fence at Graceland.

Keeping the faith, 1978.

There have been a lotta tough guys.

There have been pretenders.

There have been contenders.

But there is only one King.

BRUCE SPRINGSTEEN

1977

EPILOGUE

Elvis Presley left no autobiography; he left no definitive interview. Although there are books filled with minute details about his life and career, Elvis had little to say about his own legend. There are anecdotes and often-repeated quotes, but Elvis wrote nothing about his innermost thoughts and feelings, or his phenomenal success. For someone who has inspired so much publicity and so many biographies and news stories, Elvis himself was surprisingly silent. This may explain why Elvis means different things to different people.

Since he publicly endorsed no specific ideals or philosophy, we are free to choose the part of Elvis's legend that speaks to us. To some people he represents the ultimate rebel; to others he is a sex symbol whose performances were liberating experiences; to many people, Elvis's rock 'n' roll music was a beacon that guided their personal style. The speech writer who wrote President Jimmy Carter's statement on Elvis's death maintained that Elvis unified popular culture in America across racial and class lines. A member of the Brittish Parliament declared that Elvis did more to unite Europe after World War II than most politicians. He represented so much to so many people that only the title of "King" seems appropriate for someone of his magnitude.

What was Elvis really like? No one will ever know. In the music room at Graceland, Elvis's high-school diploma hangs among his many tributes and accolades, and friends say he was prouder of that simple document than all the awards he ever won. Elvis was a simple man who became a complex symbol.

FILMS

Love Me Tender	20th Century Fox	1956
Loving You	Paramount	1957
Jailhouse Rock	MGM	1957
King Creole	Paramount	1958
G.I. Blues	Paramount	1960
Flaming Star	20th Century Fox	1960
Wild in the Country	20th Century Fox	1961
Blue Hawaii	Paramount	1961
Follow That Dream	United Artists	1962
Kid Galahad	United Artists	1962
Girls! Girls! Girls!	Paramount	1962
It Happened at the World's Fair	MGM	1963
Fun in Acapulco	Paramount	1963
Kissin' Cousins	MGM	1964
Viva Las Vegas	MGM	1964
Roustabout	Paramount	1964
Girl Happy	MGM	1965
Tickle Me	Allied Artists	1965
Harum Scarum	MGM	1965
Frankie and Johnny	United Artists	1966
Paradise, Hawaiian Style	Paramount	1966
Spinout	MGM	1966
Easy Come, Easy Go	Paramount	1967
Double Trouble	MGM	1967
Clambake	United Artists	1967
Stay Away, Joe	MGM	1968
Speedway	MGM	1968
Live a Little, Love a Little	MGM	1968
Charro!	National General Pictures	1969
The Trouble with Girls	MGM	1969
Change of Habit	Universal	1969
Elvis—That's the Way It Is	MGM	1970
Elvis on Tour	MGM	1972

SINGLES

Ain't That Loving You Baby	1964		Don't Ask Me Why	1958
All Shook Up	1957		Don't Be Cruel	1956
All That I Am	1966		Don't Cry Daddy	1969
Almost in Love	1968		(Such an) Easy Question	1965
Always on My Mind	1972		Edge of Reality	1968
America the Beautiful	1977		The Elvis Medley	1982
An American Trilogy	1972		Faded Love	1981
Any Day Now	1969		The Fair Is Moving On	1969
Any Way You Want Me	1956		Fame and Fortune	1960
Anything That's Part of You	1962		The First Time Ever I Saw Your Face	1972
Are You Lonesome Tonight?	1960		Fool	1973
Are You Sincere	1979		(Now and Then There's) A Fool Such As I	1959
Ask Me	1964		Fools Fall in Love	1967
Baby, Let's Play House	1955		For Ol' Times Sake	1973
Big Boss Man	1967		For the Heart	1976
A Big Hunk o' Love	1959		Frankie and Johnny	1966
Blue Christmas	1957		Good Luck Charm	1962
Blue Moon	1956		Good Rockin' Tonight	1954
Blue Moon of Kentucky	1954		Guitar Man	1968
Blue River	1965		Hard Headed Woman	1958
Blue Suede Shoes	1956		Have I Told You Lately That I Love You	1957
Bosom of Abraham	1972		He Touched Me	1972
Bossa Nova Baby	1963		Heart of Rome	1971
Bringing It Back	1975		Heartbreak Hotel	1956
Burning Love	1972		Help Me	1974
Can't Help Falling in Love	1961		High Heel Sneakers	1968
Charro	1969		His Hand in Mine	1969
Clean Up Your Own Back Yard	1969		Home is Where the Heart Is	1962
Come What May	1966		(Marie's the Name) His Latest Flame	1961
Crying in the Chapel	1965		Hound Dog	1956
(You're the) Devil in Disguise	1963		How Great Thou Art	1967
Do the Clam	1965		How Would You Like to Be	1966
Doncha' Think It's Time	1958		Hurt	1976
Don't	1958		I Beg of You	1958

254

INDEX